In my films, time and place are nonsense.

SEIJUN SUZUKI

TIME AND PLACE ARE NONSENSE
THE FILMS OF SEIJUN SUZUKI

TOM VICK

Freer Gallery of Art | Occasional Papers | New Series | Volume 4

Smithsonian Institution, *Washington, D.C.*

Distributed by the University of Washington Press, *Seattle and London*

Dedicated to my father, Frank Vick, 1928–2010. He inspired me to write.

Freer Gallery of Art Occasional Papers
Original Series, 1947–1971
Interim Series, 1998–2002
New Series, 2003–

Published by the Freer Gallery of Art
and the Arthur M. Sackler Gallery

Cover: *Tokyo Drifter*, Photofest
Frontispiece: Seijun Suzuki,
Photofest

Edited by Joelle Seligson
Designed by Carol Beehler
Typeset in Scala and Scala Sans
Printed and bound in Cheverly, Maryland
by Mosaic on McCoy Silk

PHOTOS

Every effort has been made to contact copyright holders of the images, but those that have remained elusive may contact the publisher as necessary.

LIBRARY OF CONGRESS CATALOGING-IN-PUBLICATION DATA

Vick, Tom, author.
Time and place are nonsense : the films of Seijun Suzuki / Tom Vick.
pages cm – (Freer Gallery of Art Occasional Papers ; New Series, Volume 4) Includes bibliographical references and index.
ISBN 978-0-934686-33-4
1. Suzuki, Seijun, 1923—Criticism and interpretation I. Title. II. Series: Freer Gallery of Art occasional papers ; new series, v. 4.
PN1998.3.S89V53 2015
791.4302'33092--dc23
2015027037

Distributed by the
University of Washington Press
PO Box 50096
Seattle, Washington 98145-5096
www.washington.edu/uwpress

This book was supported by the Mellon Publication Endowment of the Freer Gallery of Art and by a grant from the Asian Cultural Council.

Contents

Acknowledgments

THANKS FIRST of all to my wife, Marcia Swinson-Vick, for her love and support, and to my mother, Joan Vick, for always encouraging my creative pursuits. I would also like to thank my colleagues at the Freer and Sackler Galleries who helped with advice and guidance, among them Kazuharu Ishida, Nancy Micklewright, Julian Raby, Joelle Seligson, Motoko Shimizu, Zeynep Simavi, and Jim Ulak. Thanks also to Jeremy Gleason, Kurumi Kido, and Ritsu Yoshino at the Asian Cultural Council; Yuka Sakano and Yukiko Wachi of the Kawakita Memorial Film Institute; Yoshimasa Mochizuki of the Japan Foundation; Takako Hirayama and Yuri Kubota of Nikkatsu Studios; Michael David Miller of the Humanities and Social Sciences Library at McGill University; and Todd Munson of Randolph-Macon College for the various and crucial ways they helped me with my research. For their invaluable assistance during my research trip to Tokyo, thanks to Aaron Gerow, Tatsuo Ikeda, Ichiro Kataoka, Johan Nordstrom, Tadao Sato, Mark Schilling, Ayako Uchida, Koshi Ueda, Takenobu Watanabe, Kazui Yabe, and Ayomi Yoshida. And, especially, thanks to Seijun Suzuki. ●

A Note on Japanese Words

Although in Japan family names precede given ones, I have kept with common practice in English and reversed them. Also in keeping with common practice, I eliminated the diacritics used in some Japanese names and words.

Introduction

Seijun Suzuki is an artist full of contradictions, first among them being that he refuses to consider himself an artist. Depending on who he's talking to, he's either a guy just doing his job or a prophet who can see into the future. He has performed radical experiments with film form, all the while claiming that he was just trying to make entertaining movies. His unfailing modesty—he is always quick to credit his collaborators' ideas and downplay his own—brings to mind similarly modest directors a generation older than him, such as John Ford and Howard Hawks. His films, however, were made popular worldwide by people at least a generation younger than he is. He made commercial movies, but somehow became an icon to a counterculture he couldn't bring himself to believe in. He expressed apathy about politics and ideas, yet committed scathing indictments of militarism and war to film. He exudes a relaxed, genial air, yet, in his movies, embodies the forces of nihilism and anarchy.

Suzuki has often complained about what hard work directing is, yet he continued making films well into his eighties (albeit with a couple of decade-long breaks). It is typical of his playfully self-contradictory manner that he publicly declared his retirement from filmmaking in 2006 and then attended a film market to pitch a new project in 2008. I had hoped to interview him for this book, but his health was too poor for us to meet face to face. Instead, our interactions were suitably eccentric. I sent questions by email to a friend at the Kawakita Memorial Film Institute, who translated and sent them to him, and he would respond either by postcard or through emails sent by his wife. Perhaps he is now retired for good, but you never know.

He was born Seitaro Suzuki on May 24, 1923,[1] in Nihonbashi, a district in central Tokyo, to a family in the textile trade. He was drafted into the army during World War II and twice survived having his ship sunk by American forces. After the war, he enrolled in the film department of Kamakura Academy, having failed the entrance exam for Tokyo University.

The horrors Suzuki witnessed during the war instilled in him a nihilist outlook and a deep suspicion of power and authority, which would influence his work and contribute to his sometimes strained relationships with studio bosses. He has retained a lifelong fascination with the Taisho period (during which he was born), a time of social, political, and artistic turmoil as Japan grappled with the encroachment of Western culture while torn between anarchism and militarism. The era inspired his Taisho Trilogy, three films that he released between 1980 and 1991.

He made the bulk of his films, though, in the 1960s, another tumultuous period. The border between high and low art was becoming porous: Avant-garde artists displayed their work in department stores. Suzuki's B movies—which were hardly considered highbrow cinema at the time—became

Jim Jarmusch and Quentin Tarantino, then the two coolest guys on the independent American film scene, both raved about Suzuki's work (and even blatantly ripped it off).

cult objects among the student-run "Cine Clubs," whose members were also involved in the massive political protests that swept the decade. But Suzuki is more than an avatar of the freewheeling 1960s. He is the kind of artist who both embodies and stands outside of his time, absorbing and channeling its energies into a highly individual aesthetic.

Like many other people outside of Japan, I came upon Suzuki's films in the late 1990s, when they began appearing on home video in the United States. They looked to me like they'd been made by some kind of cinematic mad scientist. They were gangster movies that seemed to mock the very concept of gangster movies, full of manic energy, visual flair, and off-kilter editing rhythms, and sprinkled with experimental techniques I had only seen in avant-garde cinema.

His films arrived on a wave of cool. A touring retrospective with the irresistible title *Branded to Thrill* preceded the video releases. The retro graphic design of the VHS and DVD boxes evoked the swinging '60s. Jim Jarmusch and Quentin Tarantino, then the two coolest guys on the independent American film scene, both raved about Suzuki's work (and even blatantly ripped it off).

His much-vaunted outlaw reputation was also an attraction. Publicity for Suzuki's films never failed to portray him as a maverick who was famously fired from Nikkatsu Studios for flaunting orders and making movies that were too outrageous for his corporate bosses. The story makes good copy and went a long way to promote his films in the West, but it has largely pigeonholed Suzuki as an eccentric B movie cult director, albeit an exceptionally talented one. As I watched his films over the years, I realized it was only part of the truth. More than a maverick bucking against his studio bosses, Suzuki was a filmmaker bucking against the movie screen itself. What I saw was a filmmaker dismantling cinema's basic illusions to create a whole new set of his own. Like many others, I wondered why it seemed that no one had heard of him before.

The West's exposure to Japanese cinema began with the refined, classically constructed films of Akira Kurosawa, Kenji Mizoguchi, and Yasujiro Ozu. Today, it is mainly divided among heirs to the classical tradition, such as Hirokazu Kore-eda and Yoji Yamada, and the gory excesses of J-Horror films and fantasy worlds of anime. Suzuki sits in a blind spot between the tradition-steeped Kurosawa, Mizoguchi, and Ozu; the politically driven avant-garde experiments of his contemporaries Shohei Imamura and Nagisa Oshima; and the postmodern genre shock tactics of current directors such as Takashi Miike and Sion Sono (who were themselves influenced by Suzuki). In the standard English-language histories of Japanese cinema, he either is absent or only briefly touched upon. Two authors of those histories, Donald Richie and Isolde Standish, saw Suzuki mainly as a symptom of the commercial and social trends of Japanese film in the 1960s. A third, Noel Burch, used him as an example of capitalism's cooptation of radical forms and ideas for commercial consumption. Somewhere in the process of fitting him into these frameworks, however, Suzuki's actual work gets lost.

That work exists in a difficult realm: a nexus between crass commercialism and artistic experimentation, between the anarchic messiness of Japanese avant-garde art of the 1960s and the "underbelly of wild and crazy art"[2] that has existed in Japan as long as the tea ceremonies and cherry blossoms more commonly associated with its traditional culture. Suzuki's admitted gaps in his knowledge of film history (foreign films were banned when he was growing up) granted him a freedom to experiment with the medium, drawing on what film critic Shigehiko Hasumi calls a "Suzukian enthusiasm" that positions him in a "peculiar place in film history."[3]

A NOTE ON APPROACH

In *Noriko Smiling*, his book on Yasujiro Ozu's 1949 film *Late Spring*, Adam Mars-Jones wrote, "Sometimes works of art need to be defended against their advocates, and great films rescued from their reputations."[4] His intent is to question Ozu's reputation in the West—established by the scholars who first wrote about him and rarely challenged since—as a Zen-influenced formalist. Instead, Mars-Jones interpreted *Late Spring* as, in part, a pointed commentary on postwar Japan, smuggled through the strict censorship of the American occupying forces. It's a persuasive new reading of the film made possible by looking at it with fresh eyes.

In a similar way, my objective with this book is to rescue Suzuki from his reputation in the West as a figurehead of "extreme" cinema. As with Ozu, this reputation is the result of our limited exposure to his work as

Suzuki sits in a blind spot between the tradition-steeped Kurosawa, Mizoguchi, and Ozu; the politically driven avant-garde experiments of his contemporaries Shohei Imamura and Nagisa Oshima. . .

well as the bulk of writing about him, which favors the extravagance of his Nikkatsu films over the complexity of his later work (and generally ignores the complexities within that extravagance). This view of him was established in the wake of the touring retrospective that first introduced him to Western audiences in the late 1990s and has rarely been challenged. My view of him is from American shores, so my intent is not to present a full portrait of his reputation in Japan, where he is as well known as a television host, writer, and all-around public personality as he is as a filmmaker. Rather, I hope to make Western audiences aware of the larger context in which he works and to explore the ways his aesthetics have infiltrated American pop culture. I will compare him to American artists of his generation who share similar sensibilities and show how his films have influenced contemporary filmmakers in America and elsewhere.

Writers such as Mars-Jones, Geoff Dyer, Gilles Deleuze, and Stanley Cavell have written lively and original books on cinema by approaching it from outside the conventions of film scholarship while employing the tools of their particular realms of expertise. This seems to me the appropriate way to approach Suzuki. To write about such an irreverent figure in the academic jargon of conventional film studies would be to risk self-parody. On the other hand, to indulge in the labored prose gymnastics and fanboy effusions that some of his commentators employ (perhaps as a way of imitating the rhythms of his films) would also be a disservice. As this book is, in part, a tribute to an artist I admire, I hope I can be forgiven for using a somewhat informal, personal tone.

I approach Suzuki as a film curator with a particular interest in filmmakers who stretch the possibilities of film language, and in the connections among cinema and other visual and narrative traditions in Asian art. In other words, I am an unashamed aesthete, not an expert in Japanese culture or the business side of the Japanese film industry. While I will include enough information on these subjects to provide context for Suzuki's life and career, those seeking deeper discussions of these topics should look to the many excellent and informative books by experts in those fields. My intention is to provide a portrait of Suzuki that is as engaging as his films are. ●

1 He changed his first name in 1957, when his directing career began to take off.

2 Tony Rayns, "The Kyoka Factor: The Delights of Suzuki Seijun," in *Branded to Thrill: The Delirious Cinema of Suzuki Seijun* (London: British Film Institute, 1995), 9.

3 Shigehiko Hasumi, "A World without Seasons," in *De woestijn onder de kersenbloesem—The Desert under the Cherry Blossoms* (Abcoude: Uitgeverij Uniepers, 1991), 15.

4 Adam Mars-Jones, *Noriko Smiling* (London: Notting Hill Editions, 2011).

TIME AND PLACE ARE NONSENSE

THE FILMS OF SEIJUN SUZUKI

1

BRANDED TO KILL AND THE "SUZUKI SEIJUN PROBLEM"

When Seijun Suzuki was summarily fired from Nikkatsu Studios in 1968, after directing some forty films in twelve years, he filed suit. His dismissal inspired public protests from not only film industry colleagues but also members of the university film societies known as Cine Clubs and everyday filmgoers, turning Suzuki into a hero for Japan's anarchic counterculture of radicalized students and artists.

It's almost impossible to imagine a director inspiring mass demonstrations for being fired by his studio today, or even in the 1960s, in the United States. And Suzuki wasn't a particularly esteemed filmmaker. His job was to turn out cheap B movies to run on double bills with the studio's more prestigious A pictures. Nor was he known as a political filmmaker. Unlike directors such as Nagisa Oshima (who was one of the driving forces behind the protests on Suzuki's behalf)[5] and Shohei Imamura, whose independent status gave them a platform to express their political outrage, he up to that point had had to work with the scripts assigned to him and stick to genre formulas. Indeed, his name was barely known outside of the student-run Cine Clubs, who were the first to appreciate the unique qualities of his work. Tadao Sato, the first major reviewer to praise Suzuki in a 1966 review of *Fighting Elegy*, only did so after hearing about him from Cine Club members and younger writers urging his magazine to write about him.

The "Suzuki Seijun Problem," as the firing, subsequent public outcry, and lawsuit came to be known, marks a moment when the trajectories of Japan's student protest and avant-garde art movements and Suzuki's increasing creative restlessness all met with an explosiveness particular to 1960s Japan. *Branded to Kill*, the film that precipitated his firing, is emblematic of that convergence. He took the elements of a standard thriller and shattered them into a succession of increasingly hysterical set pieces barely held together

Opposite: *Branded to Kill*.
Photofest

by narrative logic. It is the moment at which Suzuki's rebellious tendencies overwhelmed his training as a genre filmmaker, simultaneously torpedoing his career (if only temporarily) and vaulting him into the public eye.

Protest was, of course, already in the air. The Treaty of Mutual Cooperation and Security between the United States and Japan (abbreviated as ANPO in Japanese), which extended the American military presence, was signed in 1960 despite widespread public opposition. The artists, students, and activists who protested the treaty coalesced into a broad protest movement that grew throughout the decade. To them, Suzuki's firing was yet another example of the use of authority to crush rebellious expression. Sato, who was deeply involved in the Suzuki protests and even testified on Suzuki's behalf during the subsequent trial, told me with a chuckle that many of the artists and filmmakers who participated in the protests most likely hadn't seen Suzuki's films at all.[6] This may be so, but it was appreciation of his films from Cine Club members that drove the movement, a fact that worried industry figures, who were used to audiences passively accepting whatever they produced.

They had other reasons to be worried as well. Suzuki's most creatively productive period at Nikkatsu coincided with the Japanese film industry's steep economic decline. Film critic Shigehiko Hasumi wondered if "perhaps he even enjoyed, in a slightly anarchistic way, playing games with the only partially functioning system"[7] of a studio on its last legs.

If so, Nikkatsu's president, Kyusaku Hori, was not amused. He stoked the controversy by declaring that Suzuki made "incomprehensible films," didn't "follow the company's orders," and should quit making films and "open a noodle shop or something instead."[8] Trouble had been brewing between the two for some time. As early as 1965, Suzuki began receiving warnings from the studio for going too far. Nikkatsu was hemorrhaging money in the late 1960s, and in his 1968 New Year's speech to the staff, Hori had exhorted them to make films that were widely understandable.[9]

Suzuki's relationship with his studio bosses wasn't entirely one of the free spirit rebelling against the squares in suits. For a time, he seems to have had a real champion in Nikkatsu managing director Seijuro Emori, who Suzuki considered his "guardian angel"—even if he did ignore Emori's warnings to tone things down. Suzuki wrote:

> [Emori] had assured the head of the studio and other people at the top that I was talented. Emori was my most devoted fan, and after *Nikutai No Mon* [*Gate of Flesh*] was finished, he was the first to approach me and express his unqualified admiration. "You have caused me a lot of trouble as well, but on

the other hand, I have a princely salary thanks to you," he said, not without irony. After that, I made *Irezumi Ichidai* [*Tattooed Life*], and he kept me in check with remarks like "this is cutting it a little too close" and "you shouldn't go much further than this." I ignored his advice, and he blasted me with his criticism of my next film, *Tokyo Nagaremono* [*Tokyo Drifter*]. Shortly afterwards, Emori preceded me in being fired by Nikkatsu.[10]

The relationship between Suzuki and Hori, on the other hand, resembles some kind of slapstick double act, with Hori as the long-suffering straight man and Suzuki as his practical joke-playing sidekick. With *Tokyo Drifter*, for example, Suzuki followed the letter of the law—to deliver a low-budget showcase for actor/singer Tatsuya Watari, playing a former yakuza on the run from a gang of thugs, to sing songs—but the result completely violates the spirit. The film's escalating accumulation of gunfights and fistfights, punctuated by musical numbers, eventually overwhelms whatever storyline there was in the script with pure nonsense. According to Suzuki, the studio didn't want to release the film at all, "but they had to release it. They had nothing else to replace it with."[11] (As punishment, Suzuki was ordered to make his next film in black and white.)

Suzuki's relationship with his studio bosses wasn't entirely one of the free spirit rebelling against the squares in suits.

One of the final straws for Hori might have been a request from Kazuko Kawakita, president of a Cine Club, to borrow Suzuki's films for a retrospective, which would have marked the first time a Japanese director was so honored. Believing that honoring these "incomprehensible" movies in such a way would disgrace the company, Hori not only refused her request but withdrew all of Suzuki's films from commercial distribution. It's not clear if Hori had already decided to fire Suzuki when Kawakita made her request, but at any rate, Suzuki received notice from the studio that he wouldn't be receiving his next paycheck two weeks before the retrospective was scheduled to begin. According to Koshi Ueno, "Hori had made an example of Suzuki in order to support a restructuring of his failing company."[12]

But what was it about this filmmaker—and, more specifically, about *Branded to Kill*, an even more flagrant violation of Hori's order to make accessible films than *Tokyo Drifter*—that tapped into this cultural moment?

The plot of the film concerns Hanada (Jo Shishido), the country's "number three killer," who, after botching an assassination attempt, is pursued by the other members of his gangster syndicate. This leads Hanada to a confrontation with his nemesis, the number one killer in the country—who, it turns out, hired him for the botched job in the first place. One is tempted to see at

Fig. 1 Hanada tortured by cinema.

least a subconscious commentary, even in this bare-bones plot description, for Suzuki's increasing frustration with Nikkatsu. (When asked in an interview if he enjoyed working at the fast pace there, he replied, "It was more of a job than getting any kind of enjoyment out of making a film."[13]) A scene late in the film, in which Hanada dashes through an apartment to kick an incessantly ringing telephone while trying to stay out of a sniper's sightline, seems like an apt metaphor for the stress of working for Hori. In another scene, Hanada is tortured by cinema itself when he is shown a film of Misako (Annu Mari), the mystery woman who lured him into the assassination job, being burned at the stake while he paws at the screen (fig. 1). Throughout *Branded to Kill*, Hanada is beleaguered, pursued, and trapped.

In interviews, Suzuki generally refuses to ascribe any political meaning to his work, but that hasn't stopped people from finding social commentary in *Branded*. Daisuke Miyao asserted that the film "surely depicts the zeitgeist of Tokyo in 1967." In particular, he wrote, "the film problematizes the distinction between the bright side and the dark side of the city following the preparations for the Tokyo Olympics of 1964."

Japan had experienced tremendous economic growth in the 1960s, transforming Tokyo into a city of glossy skyscrapers. To a native like Suzuki, the city would have been entirely different from the one in which he grew up. The massive clean-up effort in the run-up to the Olympics, mandated by Japan's Minister of Health and Welfare, was primarily aimed at masking whatever unseemly elements of the old city remained. Homeless people were displaced (but not housed), bars and nightclubs were more strictly regulated, and polluted streams and canals were covered (but not cleaned up). These efforts amounted to papering over problems rather than solving them.

Fig. 2 Hanada prepares a shot.

Like the American film noirs to which it has been compared, *Branded to Kill* exposes the "dirty, vulgar and filthy things" hidden by the clean-up effort. Its violent, deranged, and lustful characters are juxtaposed against Tokyo's new, clean facades. Shishido's character "delivers all his shots in *Branded* from symbolical objects found in the modernized city."[14] He prepares one shot framed by a modern skyscraper (fig. 2) and another by aiming his gun through a massive advertising billboard. In other words, Hanada becomes an eruption of those indecent elements the authorities sought to suppress.

Stylistically, *Branded* outdoes even the increasingly eccentric films Suzuki made leading up to it. The story is linear, but the visual scheme is fragmented and off kilter. Characters are at times framed in the corners of the image, dominated by the angular structures of the strange interiors they inhabit (fig. 3). Shishido, who always seemed to deliver his most rambunctious performances for Suzuki, is at his amped-up best, and every character seems to be insane. Hanada is aroused by the smell of boiling rice. His wife (Mariko Ogawa) is almost always naked and screaming. Misako lives in a crazy

Fig. 3 Eccentric interior framing in *Branded to Kill*.

apartment full of butterflies. At any given moment, it is equally possible that a character will take off his or her clothes, shoot someone, or get shot.

In addition to his mistreatment, it must have been this sense of freedom in absurdity that drew Japan's activist students and artists to Suzuki. Post-ANPO artists rejected refinement in favor of trashier, earthier aesthetics—exactly the kind of thing that Suzuki was doing with *Branded*, a film that was "a focal point for the convergence of Japanese film noir and the Japanese avant-garde."[15]

By making a mockery of the genre film he was assigned, Suzuki ridiculed the illusions that film studios must maintain in order to sell their products. Suzuki is "a filmmaker who is aware of the limitations of film and knows how to deal with them. It goes without saying that the studio, as the instrument which tries to disguise the limitations of film permanently, feared this kind of 'ethics' most of all."[16] It came down to an irreconcilable clash between a studio in the business of creating illusions and a director determined to expose them.

The Nikkatsu affair created the legend of "Seijun Suzuki: maverick filmmaker"—a status his fans may hype a bit too much. But there's no doubt that it marks a pivotal moment in his career and sheds light on the combustible confluence of art, protest, and pop culture in 1960s Japan. For Miyao, it also "symbolizes the decline of Nikkatsu and with it the Japanese studio system and film industry as a whole."[17] Contributing to Hori's frustration was the entire film industry's economic tailspin, brought on by the increasing popularity of television, which, according to Donald Richie, "damaged the film industry much more than had either the 1923 earthquake or the 1945 fire-bombings"[18] that devastated Tokyo. Hori instituted drastic cost-cutting measures in 1968, and in 1971, the year Suzuki finally prevailed in court, Nikkatsu shut down production for three months and reopened as a porn studio. ●

5 Suzuki would return the favor by testifying on Oshima's behalf at his obscenity trial for *In the Realm of the Senses.*

6 Tadao Sato, interview with the author, Tokyo, July 31, 2013.

7 Hasumi, "A World without Seasons," 20.

8 Daisuke Miyao, "Dark Visions of Japanese Film Noir: Suzuki Seijun's *Branded to Kill,*" in *Japanese Cinema: Texts and Contexts,* eds. Alastair Phillips and Julian Stringer (London: Routledge, 2007), 194.

9 Seijun Suzuki, Paul Willemen, and Tadao Sato, *The Films of Seijun Suzuki* (Edinburgh: Edinburgh Film Festival, 1988), 40.

10 Seijun Suzuki, "The Days of Kanto Mushuku," in *De woestijn onder de kersenbloesem—The Desert under the Cherry Blossoms* (Abcoude: Uitgeverij Uniepers, 1991), 34–35.

11 Mark Schilling, *The Yakuza Movie Book* (Berkeley: Stone Bridge Press, 2003), 102.

12 Suzuki, Willemen, and Sato, *The Films of Seijun Suzuki,* 40.

13 Tom Mes, "Japan Cult Cinema Interview: Seijun Suzuki," *Midnighteye,* accessed April 20, 2015, http://www.midnighteye.com/interviews/seijun-suzuki/

14 Miyao, "Dark Visions," 197.

15 Ibid., 196.

16 Hasumi, "A World without Seasons," 23.

17 Miyao, "Dark Visions," 202.

18 Donald Richie, *A Hundred Years of Japanese Film* (Tokyo: Kodansha International Ltd., 2001), 177.

2

NIKKATSU ACTION

Founded in 1912 through a merger of four production houses and theaters, Nikkatsu is Japan's oldest film studio. Its name is a blend of *Nippon Katsudo Shashin*, which translates to "Japan Motion Pictures." In the years before World War II, Nikkatsu's roster of directors included such major figures as Shozo Makino, Kenji Mizoguchi, and Tomu Uchida. At the request of the government, it merged with two other studios, under the name Daei, during the war, while maintaining a separate distribution business under its own name. After the war, the business thrived as a distributor of Hollywood films through its network of theaters, so much so that in 1953, studio head Kyusaku Hori decided to restart production. Nikkatsu lured personnel away from the other major studios with its modern production facilities and the promise of more generous paychecks. In 1954, it began producing and releasing its own films once again.

In its 1950s–1960s heyday, Nikkatsu Studios cranked out movies at a furious pace, averaging about one a week in genres ranging from gangster movies to historical dramas. In a postwar youth market inundated with American pop culture, the studio hit upon a formula that became known as "Nikkatsu Action"—one of its most successful divisions, and the one in which Suzuki made the bulk of his films there. These films took place in a kind of fantasyland for Japanese teenagers, what Mark Schilling in his history of the genre called "a cinematic world neither foreign nor Japanese, but a mix of the two, where Japanese tough guys had the swagger, moves and even long legs of Hollywood movie heroes." Even if "they reflected mostly a thin, urban slice" of reality in a time when traditional ways still held sway in most of the country, that slice is an idealized notion of the culture of the time. It represents a rebellion against tradition dressed in the trappings of American film noir: detectives and gangsters in smart suits driving big cars, packing heat, and swilling whiskey in fancy, Western-style bars.[19]

Opposite: *The Man with a Shotgun*, see page 26.

In other words, Nikkatsu Action began as a pastiche, a not-yet-diagnosed case of postmodernism rooted less in reality than in the idealized fantasies of the Hollywood movies that the studio had distributed throughout Japan. Nikkatsu Action films digested and reinterpreted these fantasies for a domestic audience aware of, but not necessarily participating fully in, a new world of speedboats, American jazz and rock music, and Western nightclubs—luxuries that were, in reality, quite rare.

In essence, Nikkatsu Action was in the business of turning a commercial profit on the social and cultural climate of the day. It was an assembly line for bolting together sturdy little genre movies. Many of them featured its stable of handsome young male stars, marketed as the "Diamond Line" (which sounds more like luxury cars than human beings), who were rotated through the studio's quick-paced production schedule like "a baseball manager rotates his starting pitchers."[20] If the late 1950s saw "the birth of a new young hero and the development of a lighter, faster tempo in editing,"[21] the Nikkatsu method was to turn these elements into a formula.

This strategy applied not only to gangster movies, but also to a successful line of juvenile delinquent films. Two of the studio's first big hits after restarting production were Takumi Furukawa's *Season in the Sun* and Ko Nakahira's *Crazed Fruit* (both 1956). The films stirred controversy by addressing such taboo topics as adolescent sex and abortion in stories of seduction and betrayal among rich teenagers on the fashionable Shonan Coast. These innovative features—*Crazed Fruit* in particular continues to impress with its bold sensibility—launched a slew of angry youth films, tooled to appeal to teenagers as well as an older generation both scandalized and fascinated by out of control youth. According to Sato, "In the 1960s the subject most often treated in Japanese film was violence, with sex a close second."[22] The Nikkatsu Action film factory produced both in bulk.

GIRI AND *NINJO*

Though fast, cheap, and often crassly commercial, Nikkatsu Action films both influenced and were influenced by significant changes going on in Japanese culture at large. Takenobu Watanabe, who wrote a history of Nikkatsu Action (sadly not translated into English), argued that the studio broke ground by freeing its heroes from the traditional concepts of *giri* (social obligation) and *ninjo* (personal feeling). The drama inherent in these conflicting forces is the backbone of traditional Japanese drama, from Bunraku puppet theater through modern samurai and yakuza movies.[23]

Standard yakuza narratives of the time had roots in samurai stories such as the classic tale of the forty-seven *ronin* (or masterless samurai). In this apparently true story from the eighteenth century, a group of forty-seven samurai remained so loyal to their *daimyo* (feudal lord) after he was forced to commit ritual suicide that they plotted revenge for a year and eventually suffered the same fate as their master. Throughout the years, the forty-seven *ronin* have been held up as exemplars of the kind of loyalty, sacrifice, and honorable behavior considered foundational to Japanese life, particularly by traditionalists. Their story has been told in Bunraku puppet dramas and Kabuki plays and made into an opera, in addition to numerous films and television shows. Its themes provide the framework for the yakuza film genre.

In these movies, *giri* and *ninjo* emerge in the tension between a gangster or samurai's loyalty to his clan and his desire to lead an honorable life. But as traditional notions of familial obligation were beginning to erode in Japanese society in the 1950s and '60s, the focus in Nikkatsu Action films moved from the bonds of family, clan, or company to the individual. Heroes became outlaws and loners. When families are the center of Nikkatsu Action films from this era, they are usually broken. For instance, Jiro, the juvenile delinquent hero of Suzuki's *Everything Goes Wrong* (aka *The Precipice,* 1960), argues violently with his single mother's married boyfriend, then tricks him into sleeping with a teenage friend so his mother will catch them in the act. In *Young Breasts* (1958), a teenager blackmails his stepmother and tricks his girlfriend into appearing in a pornographic film. Honor and loyalty are nowhere to be found.

Though fast, cheap, and often crassly commercial, Nikkatsu Action films both influenced and were influenced by significant changes going on in Japanese culture at large.

Traditionally, the inability to reconcile *giri* and *ninjo* results in death, either by suicide or in battle. This implies that a perfect balance between the two would be a kind of utopia. The concepts' absence in Nikkatsu Action films drives their heroes to search for utopias elsewhere. They feel its absence and go in search of it.[24] One of the studio's biggest stars, Akira Kobayashi, specialized in films with wandering as a theme, including such titles as *Return of the Vagabond* (Takeichi Saito, 1960), *The Rambling Guitarist* (Saito, 1959), and Suzuki's own *Kanto Wanderer* (1963). Even the films' settings and time periods seem to roam. While set in Japan, *The Rambling Guitarist* and Suzuki's *The Man with a Shotgun* (1961) use the iconography of American westerns (fig. 4). In *Shotgun,* for instance, the hero is a wandering hunter who becomes sheriff of a lawless town after squaring off with the locals in a barroom setting that recalls the saloons of the Old West.

A similar sense of roaming individualism pervades Suzuki's *The Breeze on the Ridge* (1961), in which a rootless student meets a theater troupe, saves it from financial ruin, and then sets off on his own again, like a western gunslinger riding off into the sunset. The settings for these films evoke fictional times and places more than any actual Japanese landscape or historical period. In a discussion of *Kanto Wanderer*, Suzuki elaborated on the placelessness of Nikkatsu Action films: "They were *mukokuseki* ('borderless')—the period or the place didn't matter. Nikkatsu films were interesting that way."[25]

Kanto Wanderer was the first Suzuki film to make an impression on Koshi Ueno (who wrote a book on Suzuki's films that hasn't been translated into English), because it involved yakuza who weren't connected to a clan or boss, representing, for him, a significant move away from the standard yakuza narratives of the time.[26] Suzuki's *Tattooed Life* (1965) also is intriguing because it suggests that neither a yakuza's loyalty nor a pseudo-cowboy's wandering was entirely possible in postwar Japan. In it, a yakuza hit man is attacked by his target's bodyguard and rescued by his younger brother. The two escape and try to live normal lives elsewhere, searching, like classic Nikkatsu Action heroes, for that unattainable utopia outside the *giri/ninjo* circuit, yet drawn inevitably back into it by their shared past. What one character calls the "narrow island of Japan" won't let them go.

Fig. 4 *The Man with a Shotgun*

There is a metaphor here for Japan's societal changes after World War II. The *giri/ninjo* ethos perhaps had its uses in a society living on such a small land mass. It's impossible to roam like a cowboy in a country that would fit into a narrow slice of the American Midwest. But the exploitation of *giri/ninjo* for propaganda purposes in such films as Kenji Mizoguchi's *The Loyal 47 Ronin* (1941)—a "token effort"[27] to appease the military, which had criticized the film industry for not producing enough propaganda films—led some postwar filmmakers to reject the concepts. Mizoguchi's film "stressed the military's conception of *bushido*,"[28] the samurai warrior code that authorities evoked to encourage young men to join the military before World War II. After seeing Japan's traditions perverted to promote militarism and authoritarianism, postwar filmmakers looked for new credos to replace them—but as *Tattooed Life* implies, American-style individualism has its limits as well.

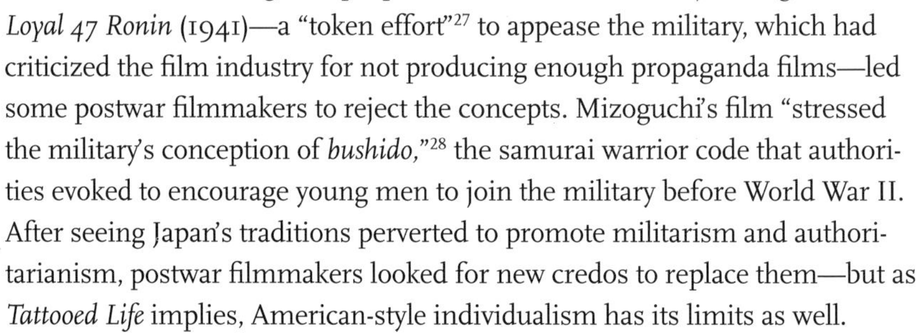

Nikkatsu was, according to Watanabe, the only studio really mining this changing cultural landscape. The appeal for audiences was Nikkatsu Action films' thrills and their new breed of heroes, who even spoke in authentic teen slang. It may be symbolic of the general return to conservatism in post-1960s Japan that Nikkatsu's decline partly owed to a new line of yakuza films, produced by Toei Studios, that returned the genre to its *giri/ninjo* roots. ●

19 Mark Schilling, *No Borders No Limits: Nikkatsu Action Cinema* (Godalming: FAB Press Ltd., 2007), 5–6.

20 Ibid., 17.

21 Tadao Sato, *Currents in Japanese Cinema* (New York: Kodansha America, Inc., 1987), 210.

22 Ibid., 229.

23 Although it hails from England, Shakespeare's *Romeo and Juliet* embodies the concept, with its stars torn between family obligation and forbidden love.

24 Takenobu Watanabe, interview with the author, Tokyo, July 29, 2013.

25 Schilling, *The Yakuza Movie Book*, 98.

26 Koshi Ueno, interview with the author, Tokyo, August 1, 2013.

27 Richie, *A Hundred Years of Japanese Film*, 97

28 Ibid.

3

LIMITS OF ILLUSION
THE DEVELOPMENT OF SUZUKI'S STYLE

THE MAKING OF A "GENRE HACK"

SUZUKI BEGAN his film career as an assistant director at Shochiku, one of Japan's oldest movie studios. It was founded in 1895 to produce Kabuki plays, and after expanding into other theatrical styles such as Noh and Bunraku, it began producing films in 1920. Shochiku was the first Japanese studio to employ actresses instead of female impersonators (a relic from Kabuki theatrical conventions), and it imported Hollywood-style production methods, including sound stages and a star system of actors and actresses. By the 1930s, the studio specialized in the *shomin-geki* genre, which portrays the lives of ordinary working-class people. It employed some of Japan's most prestigious directors, among them Yasujiro Ozu, Mikio Naruse, and Kenji Mizoguchi.

After failing the entrance exam for Tokyo University and enrolling briefly in the film department of Kamakura Academy, Suzuki went to work at Shochiku's Ofuna facility in 1946, ten years after it opened. He claims to have passed the qualification exam for assistant directors because his essay about a frustrating girlfriend amused the examiner. Suzuki described his time at Shochiku with his typical self-deprecation and irony:

> I was a melancholy drunk, and before long I became known as a relatively worthless assistant director. At a large company such as Mitsui or Mitsubishi, these things would have led to my dismissal, especially in the old days, but as the studio as well as the assistant directors themselves were laboring under the strange misconception that they were brilliant artists, almost anything was tolerated, except arson, theft and murder. So I picked flowers for my wife during working hours, and when we were on location I stayed in the bus. The job didn't pay well, but you didn't have to suck up to your superiors, and you could do whatever you wanted.[29]

Opposite: *Gate of Flesh*, see page 49.

In accordance with the apprenticeship system that Japanese film studios employed at the time, Suzuki worked under a string of directors, many of them now forgotten. In remarks typical of his insistence that directing was just a job for him, Suzuki told Koshi Ueno that he wasn't crazy about movies and that he hadn't even seen that many before starting at Shochiku: "I had seen films mostly during my childhood, not much later on ... It was quite a confusing time after the war. It was very difficult to find employment in those days. If you could get a job, you took it, no matter what it was."

He "learned the craft of filmmaking on the job."[30] Even years later, discussing the Taisho-era films he made in the 1980s, Suzuki claimed to still draw on the efficient working methods he learned at Shochiku: "Young directors nowadays shoot tremendous amounts of film. But directors trained at Ofuna studios just shot the most essential takes. There was little to choose from in the end. We were trained according to the old rules, editing took place at a very early stage, there simply wasn't that much material."[31]

He was trained in the style of the sentimental "Ofuna melodramas" for which the studio was known. Although he rarely returned to the genre, Suzuki believed that the gangster films he made at Nikkatsu varied little in structure from the melodramas he had cut his teeth on:

> I don't know all the ins and outs, but if a gangster is an outlaw, the same is true of the heroine of a melodrama, who also goes beyond conventional morality by having an impossible affair. The outlaw in melodrama is there for the female audience, the outlaw in gangster movies for the males; that's the only difference, in my opinion. I've learned how to make melodramas at the Shochiku studios in Ofuna, so I believe I've mastered all the tricks of the genre.[32]

When Nikkatsu Studios reopened in 1954 and began poaching talent from other studios, Suzuki was invited to jump ship for double his Shochiku salary. As he recalled, "The assistant directors were recruited from Ofuna studios; the technicians came from Shin-Toho." Nikkatsu developed a reputation as a place where one could move up quickly, and two years after he arrived, Suzuki became the first of the eight assistant directors recruited from Shochiku along with him to direct a movie himself.[33] From then on, he worked in Nikkatsu's B movie division, making anywhere from two to six films per year until his dismissal in 1968.

With their tight plots, terse dialogue, and crisp action scenes, even conventional B movies—Japanese, American, or otherwise—have their pleasures. While today the term has come to connote any kind of cheap genre movie, the term has roots in actual studio production practice. In the decades before television, audiences went to the movies expecting to spend several hours enjoying an array of entertainment. During the silent era, movies were accompanied by variety acts. When sound took over, those acts were replaced by shorts, newsreels, cartoons, and B movies. A similar practice was adopted in Japan, where even as late as the 1960s, films were shown on double or sometimes triple bills.

"I had seen films mostly during my childhood, not much later on ... It was quite a confusing time after the war. It was very difficult to find employment in those days. If you could get a job, you took it, no matter what it was."

Suzuki's job as a B movie director mainly was to make cheap action movies and deliver them on time and under budget. He was typically given twenty-five days to shoot a film and only three days to edit it. On *Kanto Wanderer*, for example, location scouting began on September 24, 1963; shooting ran from October 5 through November 10, and the film opened on November 16.[34]

B movie directors also had to think about their films in relation to the A movies they would accompany. Suzuki wrote:

> The B-movie director's biggest worry is the question: "What effect will the main feature have that is shown before your film?" Films from Nikkatsu almost always have the same plot: the main character falls in love with a woman, he kills the bad guy and gets the woman. This pattern is repeated in every film, so you concentrate on finding out all you can about who the actors are, who the director is, and the approach this director has. This is what the B-movie director does. For instance, the main feature's director has a habit of filming a love scene a certain way; this means that I have to handle it in another way. The director of the main feature has it easy. He doesn't have to find out how I work at all. He can just do whatever he wants. So actually a B-movie director has a harder task than his colleague who does the main feature. Because of this, the studio should give me more money than him, actually, but it's the other way around.[35]

B movies were meant to be lighter fare than the A pictures they accompanied. Before Shohei Imamura struck out independently, he too worked at Nikkatsu. Two of Suzuki's B movies were released on double bills with Imamura's A movies: *Kanto Wanderer* with Imamura's *The Insect Woman* (1963) and *Story of a Prostitute* with *Intentions of Murder* (1964). Both Imamura films are serious dramas about poverty, oppression, and cruelty. Hasumi speculated that "Suzuki's lighthearted films appealed more to the general public than Imamura's difficult, artistic style" and that they would have been relatively relaxing to watch after Imamura's more challenging films.[36]

In order to "misuse" film grammar as flagrantly as Suzuki would in his late Nikkatsu films, one must be intimately familiar with it. Averaging over three films a year for more than a decade, Suzuki mastered the quick pacing, tight plotting, and pulpy genre tropes that were the house style at Nikkatsu Action, becoming, as film critic and co-programmer of a Suzuki retrospective Tony Rayns affectionately called him, an efficient "genre hack."[37] As Rayns pointed out, "The visual and structural qualities of [Suzuki's] '60s genre films sprang from a mixture of boredom and self-preservation."[38] The scripts that Suzuki was assigned were all so similar that he had to work hard to find something in them to interest him. His stylistic experiments were, at first, intended to differentiate his work from that of other contract directors working from the same basic material.

Fig. 5 *A Colt is My Passport*

Suzuki's rise to cult fame in the West "brought the [Nikkatsu Action] genre more attention abroad, but often in a negative way, with critics hailing Suzuki as an overlooked and discarded master while dismissing the films of his colleagues as studio hack work (despite having seen few of them)."[39 40] The Japanese studio system, with its master-pupil apprenticeship program, ensured that directors and technicians received superb training. That can be seen in many Nikkatsu Action releases, such as Toshio Masuda's *Rusty Knife* (1958), a story of two gangsters trying to go straight, which features gorgeously shot nocturnal cityscapes and tense plotting. Takashi Nomura's *A Colt is My Passport* (1967), with its fractured film noir atmosphere, spaghetti western-style soundtrack, and inventive set pieces, proves that Suzuki wasn't the only director putting an eccentric and engaging personal stamp on his material (fig. 5).

High-energy rambunctiousness was the house style for Nikkatsu Action, and there are many directors who made solid work with the assignments they were given. It is no insult to them to insist that Suzuki's work was, in fact, exceptional. None of his fellows experimented as audaciously within the genre as Suzuki did, and certainly none of them made the leap into outright parody and self-reflexivity as Suzuki did with *Tokyo Drifter* and *Branded to Kill*. His firing may have made him famous for the wrong reasons, but the endurance of his films goes to show that there is more to them than the celebrity of their maker.

TESTING LIMITS

Despite the wide range of tones and styles that differentiates the phases of Suzuki's long working career, his films are linked not only by the idea of foregrounding illusion but of questioning and attacking it. Suzuki began exploring these concepts in the Nikkatsu films by divorcing elements such as lighting effects, superimpositions, camera placement, and editing rhythms from their standard purposes of furthering narrative continuity. He also experimented with separating traditional seasonal and weather symbolism from its cultural grounding—as well as with creating his own weather symbolism, using such elements as unmotivated wind effects to illustrate his characters' emotions. Beginning in his Nikkatsu phase and continuing through the later films, Suzuki engaged in repeated confrontations with the limitations of the film medium, the inevitable two-dimensionality of the screen. For him, the screen is not merely a window onto an imaginary world, but a surface to play with. At times he emphasized it as a flat plane; at others, he emphasized the artifice of what is happening behind the screen by borrowing effects from Kabuki and other forms of theater.

Hasumi posited that the "result of Suzuki's continuous investigation of the film medium is that he finds out more about its limitations than about its possibilities."[41] Rather than accepting these limitations, Suzuki plays with, pushes, and highlights them. As Suzuki wrote:

> I myself have always made films for entertainment. I believe that film is a spectacle. Arousing the spectator's curiosity, dressing up the unreal to make it look real, fooling the spectator, that's what a spectacle is all about. The spectacle is a game in which you know from the start that you are being fooled—and not a bad word about the spectator who thinks the fake is real; the one who sees the falsehood for what it is does not get angry, but laughs about the nonchalance with which he has bought his ticket.[42]

Whether or not he articulates them that way, these are avant-garde impulses in that they involve a series of experiments testing the limits of his medium. Seeing this process unfold is one of the pleasures of watching Suzuki's Nikkatsu films. Suzuki's intention with these films, according to Rayns, was "to find ways of making them more interesting to himself and his audience; an aim that would hardly be served by subverting the generic conventions on which they are built." Rather, he "brought tired material to life by discarding inessential links in the narrative structures, judiciously exaggerating other elements of the story and decorating the whole with stylized colors and boldly theatrical visual effects."[43]

EARLY EXPERIMENTS

The conventions of shot composition and editing in narrative cinema are designed to maintain the illusions Suzuki so enjoys dismantling. These conventions dictate, for instance, that the placement of the camera should follow the logic of human vision, and that every shot and cut should be motivated by the action onscreen. In a general sense, we are supposed to look at narrative films as if we are in the room with the characters. That's one of the things that makes the screen disappear and draws us into the story.

Fig. 6 *Satan's Town*

Suzuki's early films show clear signs of a director striving to be inventive by bucking against these rubrics. In *Satan's Town* (1956), the third film he directed, a near car crash is depicted using a series of freeze-frame tableaus (fig. 6), an early example of Suzuki creatively overcoming restrictions—in this case, giving the impression of a car crash without actually staging one—and startling the spectator by abruptly interrupting the movement onscreen. *Young Breasts* and *The Boy Who Made Good* (both 1958) both feature jarring, non sequitur shots of groups of feet. *Eight Hours of Fear* (1957) includes an equally bizarre passage of whip-pans across an empty landscape accompanied by jazzy music, like a demented version of Ozu's famous "pillow shots."[44]

A formal motif Suzuki often employed of juxtaposing extremely close shots with extremely long ones makes an early appearance in 1957's *Underworld Beauty*. A close-up of the manic heroine being slapped in the face cuts to a long, dizzyingly high-angled shot that places the characters in a tiny box surrounded by Tokyo's chaotic urban architecture (fig. 7, fig. 8). Experiments in scale and depth also show up in *The Boy Who Made Good*, in which Suzuki used windows in shoji screens to frame characters and create

Fig. 7 *Underworld Beauty*'s cut from a slap in a two-shot...

Fig. 8 ...to a high-angled shot dwarfing the figures in the architecture.

layers of depth. *Passport to Darkness* (1959) includes a striking use of composition-in-depth: a shot with an airplane in the background and a corpse on the tarmac in the foreground, both in sharp focus (fig. 9). In the opening shots of *Take Aim at the Police Van* (1959), highway warning signs are seen through the scope of a rifle, both situating the spectator in a murderer's point of view and announcing the cinematic danger ahead.

In *Million Dollar Smash-and-Grab* (1961), the story of two friends from the country who move to Tokyo to become professional boxers, woozy music, slow motion, and alternating one-shots are used to convey a fighter's battered mental state during a bout. These standard techniques for portraying the brutal experience of a boxing match are enhanced by Suzuki's eccentrically employed slow motion and Kabuki-like fight choreography—much less conventional tactics for representing the character's internal experience. Later in the film, Suzuki externalizes interior emotions into the film's very

Fig. 9 *Passport to Darkness*

Figs. 10, 11, 12 *The Man with a Shotgun*

mise-en-scene. After one of the boxers dies, a sudden wind lashes the boxing studio, as if nature itself were expressing his friend's grief.

In *The Man with a Shotgun* (1961), Suzuki cuts between two characters as they argue, keeping them in sharp focus through a crowd that remains blurry. This blur is caused by opening the camera lens's aperture to reduce the depth of field, a technique used to compensate for lack of light or to focus the audience's attention on a particular area of the screen. It usually implies distance in a scene. I've never seen it used in such a playfully unorthodox way, as in this case it implies somehow that the center of the room is permanently blurry while the distant edges remain sharp (fig. 10, fig. 11). In another scene from that film, Suzuki created eccentric compositions by reflecting a character in a mirror on his desk (fig. 12).

During a strange fight scene in *A Breeze on the Ridge,* one character throws colored liquids at his opponent. They cause the screen to glow in their respective hues as they make impact, leaping from the diegetic space of the film to actually tint the screen itself (fig. 13). Suzuki claims that the idea "just hit me. After all, we had to think of something. We didn't plan everything in advance. We weren't as calculating as Kurosawa or Ozu."[45]

Suzuki often uses such nonchalance to deflect questions about his techniques. Nonetheless, we can see in *Breeze* and *Shotgun* examples of his interest in the surface of the screen. In *Breeze,* the screen becomes a solid, though transparent, object that can be impacted by forces. In *Shotgun,* it becomes malleable through a narrow depth of field employed purely for effect.

Suzuki's fondness for using standard techniques and effects in the "wrong" ways is especially apparent in his increasingly unorthodox use of superimpositions in his late 1950s and early '60s films. One of the earliest special effects, superimpositions are often used in traditional narrative cinema to express characters' inner lives: to make visible the thoughts, memories, dreams, or hallucinations inside their heads. One example is a scene in Buster Keaton's *Neighbors* (1920), in which a father examines the wedding ring bought by his prospective son-in-law while the words "Acme 5 and 10 Cent Store" appear superimposed onscreen, indicating his opinion of the financial means of his daughter's wooer. Another occurs in Alfred Hitchcock's *Vertigo* (1958), when the hero has a nightmare about falling and his body is superimposed descending over rooftops.

Fig. 13 The screen turns green when liquid splashes a character in *The Breeze on the Ridge*

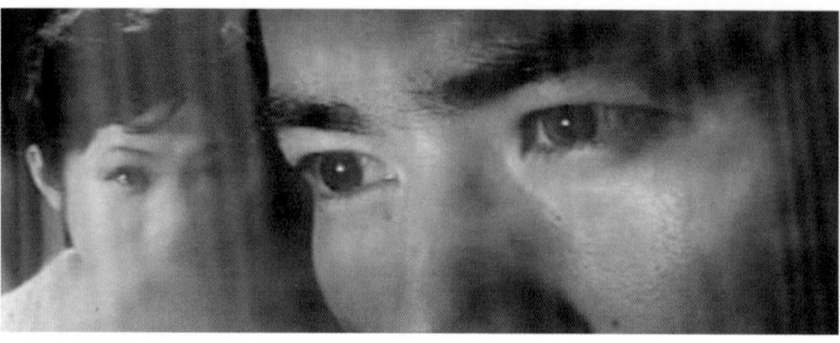

Top: Fig. 14 *Young Breasts*
Above: Fig. 15 *Passport to Darkness*

Suzuki at first used superimposition effects conventionally. In *Young Breasts*, for instance, a woman remembers two men who wrote to her and their images appear on the letters she holds (fig. 14). When the hero's wife is murdered while he was out drinking in *Passport to Darkness* (1959), he must try to piece together his memories of that night. The events appear superimposed on screen as he narrates them (fig. 15).

But even as early as 1960's *The Sleeping Beast Within*, we can see Suzuki playing around with superimposition techniques. The plot concerns a woman who, with the help of a reporter, goes in search of her missing father, who may be involved in criminal activity. In one scene, as a bargirl recounts a night with the missing man, she is superimposed over the remembered scene and turns around to watch it (fig. 16). As with the mirror scene in *The Man with a Shotgun* and the colors tinting the screen in *A Breeze on the Ridge*, this is an early example of Suzuki emphasizing the screen's two-dimensionality by inserting another screen within it, creating a second flat plane.

In *The Sleeping Beast Within*, the father returns and recounts the criminal activities he was involved in during his disappearance. In a reversal of standard practice, his memories are superimposed not on him but on his stunned interlocutors. In the flashback that the father narrates, he appears

Fig. 16 *The Sleeping Beast Within*

Fig. 17 *The Sleeping Beast Within*

at the bottom of the screen, tiny against their looming faces, which are filmed close up and from a low angle to emphasize their disapproval (fig. 17). Superimpositions are not an uncommon way to portray flashbacks, but it is rare to have the characters in the scene actually watch them, as they do in these two examples. In this, they can be seen as preludes to Suzuki's even more radical use of the technique in *Gate of Flesh* (1964).

SUZUKI'S BREAKTHROUGH: THE LATE NIKKATSU FILMS

Suzuki, amazingly, had some two dozen B movies under his belt before 1963, the breakthrough year when he started collaborating with art director Takeo Kimura—to whom, with typical modesty, Suzuki attributes his bold leap in style in the mid-1960s. Kimura's background in theater design was crucial for designing creative sets on shoestring budgets, and many of the avant-garde visual flourishes in Suzuki's films can be attributed to Kimura's experience in experimental theater. So close a collaborator was Kimura that he even received screenwriting credit on several titles, including *The Flower and the Angry Waves* (1964), *Capone Cries a Lot* (1985), and (as part of the group pen-named *Guryu Hachiro*[46]) *Branded to Kill*.

As Suzuki put it, "It was with Kimura that I began to work on ways of making the fundamental illusion of cinema more powerful."[47] I might change that last word to "palpable" or "visible," or expand it to "more powerful than the story it's meant to serve." In the bulk of Suzuki's films from 1963 on, compositional strategies are often unstuck from conventional narrative logic. Effects such as superimpositions and lighting changes can burst hysterically onto the screen from inside his characters' consciousness in ways that owe

Figs. 18, 19 *Detective Bureau 2-3: Go To Hell, Bastards!*

little to traditional cinematic construction. He had been working with cinematographers Shigeyoshi Mine and Kazue Nagatsuka off and on for several years by then. The addition of Kimura fired the creativity of all four men and led to Suzuki's most creatively fertile period at Nikkatsu.

Even before Kimura came aboard, *Detective Bureau 2-3: Go to Hell Bastards!* (1963), with its explosive opening shots of a Pepsi delivery truck spewing bullets; flat, bright color scheme (a signature of Mine's style); and experiments with scale and depth, began to synthesize Suzuki's first flashes of individuality. In this action movie starring Jo Shishido (in his first Suzuki film) as a cop on the hunt for stolen weapons, we can see Suzuki thinking more fully about giving his shots punch and visual interest. In one scene, a character's fractured mental state is made visible by showing her delivering a monologue into a broken mirror (fig. 18). In others, he frames the action from extremely high or low vantage points with tremendous depth of field, reducing the actors who are ostensibly the focus of the action to tiny background figures (fig. 19).

In addition to being visually striking, these two examples bring attention to the surface of the screen in nearly opposite ways. In the first, it is shattered into fragments. In the other, the long depth of field emphasizes the pictorial elements of the frame over the figures within it, drawing our eyes to the angles and shapes these elements form rather than to the characters at the center of the story.

Kanto Wanderer is indeed as "borderless" as Suzuki claimed, but its plot does nod to the classic yakuza *giri/ninjo* conflict. Akira Kobayashi's character Katsuta is torn between a doomed romance with married cardsharp Tatsuko and a debt of honor to his boss. Kimura's contribution is evident in theatrical lighting effects used to project the characters' motives and emotions in ways that depart radically from the norm. As Stephen Teo put it, "Rather than to signal the passing of time, lights darken and brighten to show the changing

Fig. 20 *Kanto Wanderer*

emotions of the characters without regards to the natural behaviour of light."[48] In the gaming room where she deals cards, Tatsuko is lit brightly and framed against a dark window, causing her to stand out from the gamblers around her. The light on her has no discernible source, but functions rather like a theater spotlight, emphasizing her loneliness in a roomful of shadowy strangers (fig. 20). During an intense conversation between Katsuta and Tatsuko, the entire lighting scheme of the room changes with no regard to the light

Left: Fig. 21 *Kanto Wanderer*: As two characters talk...

Right: Fig. 22 ...the light changes with no natural motivation.

coming in through the window or the light sources shown in the room, but instead projecting the characters' charged emotions (fig. 21, fig. 22).

Spectacular, nontraditional uses of color also pervade the film. During another confrontation, the sky visible through the window behind Katsuta and Tatsuko rapidly changes from orange to yellow to blue to violent purple, vaguely mimicking the colors of a sunset—but, in Suzuki's expressionistic scheme, the purpose is to render visible the couple's strong, conflicted feelings. Suzuki also used red and white as a symbolic motif, illustrating the yakuza code of honor: red for prison, white for death. Another director might have confined himself to merely weaving these colors into the decor or costumes. Suzuki staged a final battle during which the walls of a room fall away to reveal a field of solid red (fig. 23, fig. 24); the scene then cuts to Katsuta walking through white snow (fig. 25) in a pure black space.

This is Suzuki pushing against the demands of narrative in a much more significant way than he did in previous films. Light, colors, and even the set itself call attention to themselves by refusing to behave naturally. They perform functions other than what we expect them to do in a film. Lights don't just illuminate the actors; they project their emotions. Colors announce themselves as symbolic, and the set, which the viewer is meant to believe is the world in which the characters live, actually falls apart, exposing its artifice. The very mechanisms designed to further the cinematic illusion are now being used to expose it.

An enigmatic quote from Suzuki on the use of snow imagery in *Kanto Wanderer* confirms something Ayako Uchida, the script supervisor for many of his films, told me in an interview.[49] Suzuki often kept his actors in the dark about his motivations behind a scene, lest their awareness of the symbolism he intended cause them to play it up too much. He wrote, "The snow resembles their inner world. On the set, though, they must not be aware of the snow. Their only concerns are gambling and killing. The snow must fall silently, far away, both transcending and containing the action."[50] Elsewhere he remarked of this scene, "If this were some absurd experimental movie, it would be all too easy to push [the actors] into the background while foregrounding the snow, making it an explicit symbol of their inner world. What I'm talking about is entirely different. It snows because something has to happen in that place."[51]

Note that he didn't say it had to snow because it was wintertime. Indeed, as Shigehiko Hasumi's close reading of this film shows (in an essay appropriately titled "A World without Seasons"), the snow scene is part of Suzuki's systematic deconstruction of traditional Japanese nature symbolism. He

Fig. 23 *Kanto Wanderer*: Katsuta's opponent stumbles toward the shoji screens...

Fig. 24 ...which fall away to reveal a field of red...

Fig. 25 ...and the scene cuts immediately to Katsuta in an abstract snowstorm.

heightened the sense of unreality and artificiality by decoupling seasonal symbols from the seasons themselves, thus subverting any attempt to interpret the film in relation to how such symbolism is expected to be deployed. As Hasumi wrote:

> The signs that refer to winter, summer and fall are completely disconnected from the natural sequence of the seasons. In a landscape that has nothing wintry about it, it suddenly starts to snow very heavily. At that point, the yakuza hero ... commits a murder in the back of an illegal gambling den. And when, shortly afterwards, the proprietress of the gambling den, seated on her balcony, thinks of him, her lover who turned himself in after the murder and who is now in prison, we hear the dry sound of wind chimes in the vestibule. These masterly scenes will impress the spectator, but give him a sense of alienation. In Japan, wind chimes have always been regarded as one of the typical sounds of summer. Is summer approaching, then, even though it is still snowing? We have hardly asked ourselves this, when Suzuki baffles us with a second series of peculiar scenes. From the vestibule, we see the smoke of brushwood burning in the distance. The literary tradition of seasonal words in haiku prescribes that this is a symbol of autumn. The dry tinkling of wind chimes that, during hot Japanese summers, gives the illusion of coolness, in the same shot as the burning of brushwood. What does this mean? How are we to interpret this jumble of seasons, in which apparently disconnected symbols of summer, fall and winter are shown within a few minutes? When I point out the incongruity of these details, I certainly do not intend to criticize Suzuki's ability as a filmmaker. As I have remarked before, this is exactly what typifies him as an auteur. He consciously chooses to show this jumble of seasons to prevent the unfolding of the story line being hindered by a sentimental ode to nature and its attendant symbolism.[52]

This is in keeping with what Hasumi identified in Suzuki's work as his ruthless insistence that dramatic impact come from purely cinematic elements. The tactic involves removing from his films any non-cinematic cues, such as the seasonal symbolism so deeply ingrained in Japanese culture that it is often used as a form of shorthand to trigger emotional responses or signal plot points. Hasumi pointed to one of Japan's most iconic films, Kurosawa's *Seven Samurai* (1954), as an example of this:

> The heavy rainfall ... that breaks loose at the climax of the film unmistakably refers to the rainy season. For the Japanese viewer, who is familiar with this

kind of symbolism, it is clear that this is the moment when the battle will be decided, and that the film will end shortly with the ritual of the harvest. With this, he gives significance to the moral victory of the farmers over the samurai. There is a continuous connection between the story line and the changing of the seasons.

Hasumi described this connection as a weakness, an indication that Kurosawa lacked confidence "in the action inherent in the story" and resorted to traditional seasonal cues as a kind of crutch. By contrast, traditional seasonal symbols such as falling snow and cherry blossoms, while present in Suzuki's films, "have no relationship whatsoever to the seasons." Hasumi continued:

> Suzuki does not even allow a shadow to fall. The reason for this is that he wants to prevent the symbolism of the season to interfere [sic] with the flow of the film. The Japanese have a strong emotional bond with the seasons, which is expressed in the literary tradition of haiku. Suzuki wants to turn away from the Japanese way of experiencing nature: he creates distance, by showing exaggerated images of nature. ... In keeping with their dramatic impact, he uses snow as a symbol of permanent things, rain as a symbol of things that fall away and cherry blossoms as a symbol of things that are blown away by the wind.

In other words, Suzuki uses these elements as symbols in themselves, with meanings assigned by him, rather than references to extra-cinematic influences.[53] When asked why he didn't follow the order of the seasons in his films, Suzuki responded with typical absurdity: "Well, the order of the seasons is all wrong! Summer should come first, and then spring. As long as you stick to the order of the seasons, people will go see your films and the cash register will ring."[54]

Hasumi also noted a subversion of seasonal symbolism in the opening shot of *Youth of the Beast* (1963). The scene is in black and white but for a single red camellia blossom, which "destroys the seasonal symbolism. This camellia has no psychological meaning whatsoever, and also has nothing to do with the camellia of which it is said that it announces the cold at the beginning of spring. The only purpose of its redness seems to be to incite action."[55]

Youth is another good example of Suzuki stripping the narrative down to its bare bones in order to foreground formal invention. Howard Hampton

"Well, the order of the seasons is all wrong! Summer should come first, and then spring. As long as you stick to the order of the seasons, people will go see your films and the cash register will ring."

Fig. 26 *Youth of the Beast*

surmised that the Haruhiko Oyabu novel on which *Youth* is based had a more elaborate plot inflected with psychological motivations for the characters, which Suzuki doesn't "so much abandon as fast-forward through, saving what plays well, ditching the interstices that connect the A-to-B-to-C dots."[56] For this reason, the film's many double and triple crosses can be difficult to follow, but maybe, after twenty-seven films, it was dawning on Suzuki that the oft-recycled plots of B movies mattered as little to the audience as they did to him. As he once said, "Films from Nikkatsu usually have the same plot: the main character falls in love with a woman, he kills the bad guy and gets the woman. The pattern is the same in every film."[57]

Jo Shishido plays a disgraced ex-cop, recently released from prison, who exacts revenge on two rival gangs for the death of the one colleague who stood by him. Although the film is hardly pure invention—the demands of narrative, however stripped-down, wouldn't permit it—it differentiates itself from Suzuki's previous movies when it abruptly bursts from a black-and-white (but for that camellia) first scene into garish color for the remainder of the film. Everything, from the color schemes to the acting to the choice of camera angles, is keyed to maximum intensity, and the action scenes are conceived and performed with more verve than in earlier films. Toward the grand finale, Shishido gets into a gunfight while hanging upside down from the ceiling (fig. 26).[58]

Shishido's character is first encountered on a post-prison carouse in a swank nightclub, where the gangsters who own the joint observe him through a huge one-way mirror (fig. 27), a detail that was not in the original script. Hasumi saw in this mirror a metaphor for Suzuki's exploration of the screen as an undeniably two-dimensional surface where depths are illusionary—a reason why this film is regarded as one of his creative breakthroughs. Hasumi called it "a story that's intended to play games with the spectator who is trying to determine the proper distance. This spectator will have the cruel fate of always being left behind in the shallow surface layer of the film. ... The spectator is an incorrigible creature who allows himself to be fooled time and time again. And that is precisely the discovery that Suzuki makes with [*Youth of the Beast*]. Film exists only by virtue of the two dimensional screen."[59]

Suzuki continued to use glass surfaces and other forms of screens that create flat yet deep spaces throughout his career.[60]

Suzuki's emphasis on the two-dimensionality of the screen partly accounts for the increasingly avant-garde qualities of his films beginning with *Youth*, even if he may have regarded these impulses simply as ways to make better action movies. Hasumi grappled with these contradictions:

> Suzuki's world, in which everything is surface and action is pure, seems barely concrete. ... The work of the craftsman Suzuki gradually evolved towards a kind of avant-garde. Not because he had had enough of ordinary films. He wanted to give films a new lease on life with action and suspense, two elements that, in his view, had suffered because of formalized repetition and psychological obscurantism. He kept stressing that point up to [*Branded to Kill*]. What is important is that this well thought-out consistency did not lead to maturity, but confronted him with the limitations of film. Suzuki himself doesn't see his films of this period as abstract at all. Rather, he believes they're extremely concrete quests for the essence of action films. ... This, probably, is where the brutal contradictions come in. The pure action shown on the "surface" is precisely the film's most concrete mode of existence. And when it reaches real concreteness, the film becomes abstract and the medium has to believe in its own limitations.[61]

Youth also is an early example of Suzuki borrowing techniques from the stage in order to test the limits of cinematic illusion. When Shishido is summoned from his table to meet with the gangsters, he crosses the frame just as the lights dim for a fan-dancer's performance, playfully employing the theatrical technique of using a lighting change to indicate a new scene. The "cor-

Fig. 27 The one-way mirror in *Youth of the Beast*

Fig. 28 *Youth of the Beast*: Note the lavendar curtain in contrast to the yellow windstorm.

rect" way to handle such a transition in film would be through a cut or a fade. Creating a transition through a theatrical lighting change heightens the artifice of the scene and wittily foregrounds Shishido as just as much a theatrical performer as the fan dancer. Suzuki would borrow techniques from the stage more heavily in *Gate of Flesh*, but the idea emerged here.

In perhaps *Youth*'s most famous scene, Suzuki employed blatantly unrealistic, garish color and one of his signature wind effects to create atmosphere and project characters' moods. As an uncanny dust storm rages outside, a sadistic yakuza boss whips his mistress on a blood-red carpet, then chases her outside and assaults her in the raging yellow landscape until their forms dissolve into the dust (fig. 28). Shishido's character watches all this while framed by the room's lavender curtains, which provide a dissonant counterpoint to the dominant yellow (purple being, in color theory, the opposite of yellow).

Though less inventive overall than *Youth of the Beast, The Call of Blood* (1964) contains one formally daring scene in which Suzuki flagrantly misused a common technique to create emotional effect through purely cinematic means. Two brothers struggling against their yakuza family ties argue while driving through a rainstorm. It was standard practice at the time to shoot such a scene by having the actors sit in a stationary car and using rear projection to give the illusion of the landscape passing by, an effect that looks strange today and probably did even then. But instead of showing the road unfurling behind them, Suzuki showed violent ocean waves. This makes no narrative or visual sense, but it serves to emphasize the preposterousness of rear projection and, in keeping with Suzuki's style, to make visible the brothers' roiling emotions (fig. 29).

Fig. 29 *The Call of Blood*

Kimura's theatrical design training came in especially handy on *Gate of Flesh*, the story of a group of prostitutes whose hideout is invaded by Shintaro (Jo Shishido), a veteran on the run from the law. The sets, which evoke but don't attempt to replicate postwar Tokyo, were made from scrap plywood that Kimura scavenged around the studio lot and painted with a cheap wash in dull colors, emphasizing the women's colorful dresses (fig. 30). As Kimura put it, Suzuki's permission to make unrealistic sets freed him to create a theatrical look.[62] The actors, too, were encouraged to act more theatrically than cinematically, with loud voices and broad gestures. There is even a passage of soliloquies delivered by each of the female characters, sitting or standing alone in abstract settings color-coordinated with their dresses, delivered as if to a theater audience (fig. 31). Usually this kind of acting doesn't play well in movies, but in *Gate of Flesh* it works with the sets and similarly theatrical lighting to make a kind of B movie theater of the absurd.

Even more than in previous films, Suzuki used superimpositions to eccentric ends in *Gate of Flesh*. In an early scene, when Maya (Yumiko Nogawa), the new girl in the gang, first lays eyes on Shintaro, a small superimposition of him with a devil mask on his head appears. It turns out to be

Fig. 30 *Gate of Flesh*: colorful dresses pop against the drab background.

Fig. 31 A soliloquy in *Gate of Flesh*

Fig. 32 *Gate of Flesh*: Shintaro is superimposed beside a chacter he is actually facing.

Fig. 33 *Gate of Flesh*

Fig. 34 *Gate of Flesh*: He runs through the street while she "watches" via superimposition.

Fig. 35 *Gate of Flesh*

foreshadowing: she tells him later that he reminds her of a boy from her childhood who wore such a mask in a play. In a scene in which Shintaro and a woman argue in a small room, they are seen superimposed on one another, facing the screen frontally although in reality they are facing each other (fig. 32). This extremely unorthodox staging method is repeated later in the film when Shintaro sits in a restaurant, facing another character from across the room, and we see them both superimposed frontally (fig. 33). In the earlier scene, when Shintaro leaves, pursued by the police, the woman "sees" him running through the streets (fig. 34).

These deliberate misuses of superimposition effects still project a character's inner thoughts. Many of the instances are associated with Maya, the main female character. When a fellow prostitute is tortured by her cohorts for the crime of falling in love, we see Maya superimposed on the scene, looking worried because she is committing the same unpardonable act by falling for Shintaro (fig. 35). Whenever she thinks of him, he appears in superimposition. But even if some of these examples have conventional motivations, visually they are quite unusual.

Much has been made of the fact that each prostitute wears a specific color of dress throughout the film, with the general reading being that the colors symbolize their personalities. Suzuki is notoriously hard to pin down in interviews,[63] and on the *Gate of Flesh* dress question, he has given different answers at different times. In one interview, he said that the colors have no meaning, that he brought in the bright, monochrome dresses out of "desperation" because they popped against the set's drab colors better than the patterned dresses available from the costume department. Interpretations of their symbolism—which he calls "strained"—only came from others later on.[64]

In another context, however, he directly contradicted himself, explaining, "In my symbolic system, green represents peace and calm: red stands for sudden eruptions and fear; yellow stands for niceness and compromise; and purple for inner revulsion." He stated that he dressed Maya in peaceful green ("I shot her as if some mystic had shrouded her in a green veil") because "if there hadn't been a war, Maya would have been an ordinary young woman."[65] When Maya is tortured by the other women for the grievous offense of falling in love with Shintaro, a green fog appears on both sides of the screen—matching the dress she was wearing before her tormentors stripped her naked (fig. 36)—as if the last vestige of her innocence is dissipating.

Fig. 36 *Gate of Flesh*: Mist the color of Maya's dress suffuses the scene.

Fig. 37 *Tattooed Life*

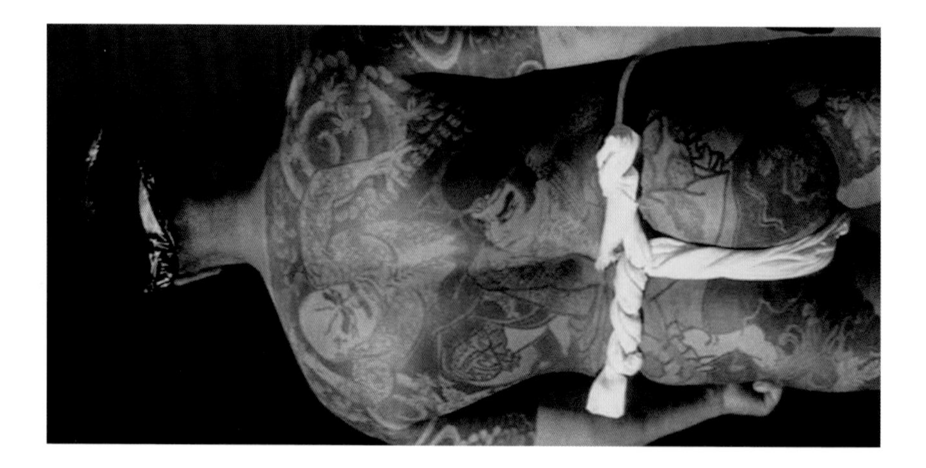

On the other hand, Suzuki could have been misleading both interviewers. The bright yellow that bathes the violent rape scene in *Youth of the Beast*, for instance, can hardly stand for "niceness and compromise." (And yellow is explicitly the color of death in his 2001 film *Pistol Opera*.)

Tattooed Life (1965), the film for which Suzuki was chastised for "going too far," opens with shots of tattooed yakuza. Though they are standing, the men are filmed sideways in order to emphasize the widescreen format (fig. 37)—a foreshadowing of its final fight scene, in which the surface of the screen becomes an important formal device. This scene includes Suzuki's most flagrant violation of the rules of camera placement. It features a shot from below the floor, as if it had suddenly become transparent—an angle from which it is literally impossible to see (fig. 38). When Alfred Hitchcock pulled a similar trick in *The Lodger* (1931), it was motivated by the scene's action: people were listening to someone walking around on the floor above

Fig. 38 The suddenly invisible floor in *Tattooed Life*

Figs. 39, 40 *The Lodger*

them (fig. 39, fig. 40). But in Suzuki's version, there is no motivation. Hasumi attributed this inventiveness to the "Suzukian Enthusiasm" that comes from the director's lack of influence from forebears such as Hitchcock. This is partly because foreign films were banned when Suzuki was growing up and partly, perhaps, due to his own apparent indifference to them, which frees him from the burden of influence and allows him to experiment. "When he has a floor of glass put in, to shoot the actors from below, this is no reference to Hitchcock. ... [He] wants to place his camera under a glass floor simply because he had never seen such things before."[66]

This is not to say that "Suzukian Enthusiasm" has no aim or purpose. The floor can disappear because it is an illusion. What is real is the screen, in all its two-dimensionality, and this is what draws our attention. In another striking sequence in *Tattooed Life*, just before the fight scene, the hero passes through a succession of sliding shoji screens. These screens function as a series of planes

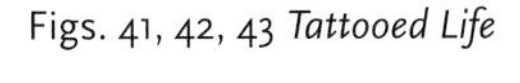

Figs. 41, 42, 43 *Tattooed Life*

parallel to the movie screen (fig. 41, fig. 42, fig. 43). Each depth he approaches becomes another flat surface, echoing the flatness of the screen itself.

In his 1966 film *Fighting Elegy*, about a violent young teenager's indoctrination into militarist ideology during the Sino-Japanese War, Suzuki reinterpreted one of Japan's most cherished symbols: the cherry blossom. Traditionally, the cherry blossom represents spring, renewal, and the transience of life. During their brief period in bloom, it is customary in Japan to celebrate with parties under the cherry trees, enjoying food, drink, and the beauty of the blossoms. But in *Fighting Elegy*, a battle, rather than a picnic, takes place under a cherry tree because, in Suzuki's personal symbology, cherry blossoms represent war.

In keeping with his impish public personality, Suzuki once conducted an interview with himself, which he then published in his 1980 book *Lonely Reflections*. The first question he asked himself is about cherry blossoms. He responded by saying that the "first association when I see cherry blossoms is battle, war. ... The cherry blossom has different associations for each person, but as a director I'm not so much looking for meaning or connections, but rather for settings that fit the feeling of certain events." He recalled a novel that describes "how a cherry tree flowers more richly and beautifully than before because it extracts nourishment from a dead body buried under it. ... To my mind, no other flower symbolizes death and dying than the cherry blossom, because mortality and nihilism loom behind its beauty."[67]

Snow, too, is used in *Fighting Elegy* to further Suzuki's aesthetic aims rather than to evoke seasonal symbolism. At the end of the film, snow falls as its young hero departs for Tokyo to join the military. Hasumi wrote, "In spite of the snow piling up, the action in this film is not obscured by the seasons. By avoiding at all costs to make [sic] a statement about the seasons, Suzuki emphasizes the inalienable right of the author to determine action and movement himself."[68]

Similarly, the sudden winds that seem to come out of nowhere in Suzuki's films are part of a symbolic system of his own devising. They externalize characters' emotions (as in *Million Dollar Smash-and-Grab*) and emphasize their powerlessness in the hands of fate. A sudden, irrational wind kicks up during the battle under the cherry blossom tree in *Fighting Elegy*, and wind gusts figure prominently in *Story of a Prostitute* (1965). By this point in his career, Suzuki was so in sync with his collaborators Kimura, Mine, and Nagatsuka that the latter was able to predict when the director would use these wind effects. Suzuki remarked that, in *Story of a Prostitute*, "there was nothing about wind in the script. But Nagatsuka was way ahead of me.

[Nagatsuka said]: 'Either the people are sad, poor, miserable, nasty or ridiculous, or they show themselves to be stronger than the wind, as if they are rebelling against God.' "[69] In this story of a forbidden affair between a soldier and a comfort woman on the front during the Sino-Japanese War, the wind turns the characters' rebellion against authority into a metaphor for rebellion against God. This underscores a theme that runs through both *Story of a Prostitute* and *Fighting Elegy*: the wartime ideology enforced by the Japanese government in the years before World War II was so all-encompassing that rebelling against it was as futile as rebelling against fate.

Carmen from Kawachi (1966) is a picaresque story of a young woman from the country who moves to Osaka and eventually Tokyo, becoming embroiled in prostitution, exploitation, and eventually vengeance and murder along the way. Suzuki employed an array of cinematic effects divorced from diegetic logic to convey the heroine's heightened emotions. Her female boss invites Carmen to live at her house and then attempts to seduce her. The next day, the boss sleeps with a male friend upstairs while a now very confused Carmen wanders around downstairs; roving theatrical spotlights project her bewilderment. Late in the film, during a monologue in which Carmen rails against the many men who have abused her, Suzuki broke the action into a series of jarring freeze frames that function much like visual exclamation points punctuating her speech.

Fig. 44 *Carmen from Kawachi*

Carmen also employs glass surfaces to emphasize the surface of the screen. An argument the heroine has with a customer she slept with is framed next to a rotating mirror that repeatedly brings his reflection in and out of the shot, emphasizing, as mirrors tend to do in Suzuki's visual schemes, the surface of the movie screen by highlighting the man's presence on the other side of it (fig. 44). Later, her boyfriend dies, and Carmen attaches mementos of him to a glass wall—telling a story through images on a flat surface, like the film itself.

FINAL STRAWS: *TOKYO DRIFTER* AND *BRANDED TO KILL*

Suzuki's habit of altering the scripts he was given to maximize action and spectacle, at times even at the expense of narrative coherence, reached an apex of absurdity in *Tokyo Drifter*, which is surely the most wacko entry in the Nikkatsu Action lone hero films. Suzuki's tongue must have been planted firmly in his cheek when he said that he'd complied with Nikkatsu and toned things down after being told he'd gone "too far" with *Tattooed Life*.[70]

Fig. 45 The high-contrast look of expired film stock in *Tokyo Drifter*

Tokyo Drifter begins with a gesture more at home in experimental than commercial cinema: grainy, high-contrast, black-and-white opening scenes that were shot on expired film stock. Suzuki had no idea how they would come out. The effect becomes unstuck from the narrative, emphasizing film as a conveyor of illusions as well as a physical substance subject to decay and manipulation (fig. 45). The film's Rube Goldbergian plot—featuring singing idol Tatsuya Watari as Tetsu, a yakuza who tries to leave the life of crime behind and become a drifter—is basically a Maguffin, a way for Suzuki to bolt a series of bizarre set pieces to what is essentially an American western plot (complete with saloon brawl). Tetsu, in a tacky, powder-blue suit, attempts to evade various mobs of thugs through a succession of increasingly abstract settings that have little connection to one another. Nikkatsu wanted to use the film as a vehicle for its title song, so Suzuki was "told to put it in as much as possible. When you are using a song like that, the story ceases to matter."[71] Working with a reduced budget as punishment for *Tattooed Life*, Suzuki and Kimura cobbled together sets that are at once minimal and baroque. They reach their apex in a final battle scene, which takes place in a vast white room dominated by a huge donut-shaped sculpture that changes color as the action rages (fig. 46, fig. 47).

Tokyo Drifter is so nonsensical that it has to be a deliberate attempt to undermine the gangster film. Tony Rayns' contention that Suzuki never subverted genre material may apply to the films that came before, but not to this one. Nikolaus Vyrzidis summed it up well: "With influences that range from Pop Art to 1950s Hollywood musicals, and from farce and absurdist comedy to Surrealism, Suzuki shows off his formal acrobatics in a film that is clearly meant to mock rather than celebrate the yakuza film genre."[72]

Isolde Standish saw the film as subversive both because it mocks the way yakuza films traditionally portray their gangster heroes as chivalrous and

Fig. 46 *Tokyo Drifter*

Fig. 47 *Tokyo Drifter*: Note the changing color of the “donut” sculpture.

honorable, and because it explicitly connects the dots between the crime and business worlds. Of Suzuki's gangster films in general, she wrote, "By filling in the historical detail and linking the films to the realities of corporate corruption evident in the media of the day, his films lost their sense of ambiguity, becoming subversive."[73] This subversiveness appealed to the student activists who followed his work while alienating "the more conservative middle-class salaryman," chief among them being Nikkatsu boss Kyusaku Hori.

By contrast, *Branded to Kill*'s narrative holds together surprisingly well considering the chaos of which it is constructed. We know who the assassin Hanada is trying to kill, who is trying to kill him, and why, and there are distinct goals that are literally enumerated by the characters' ranks within the assassins' organization. But this too comes across as parody. Why bother with traditional motivations for characters when you can just give each of them a number and a gun and let them have at it?

If, in other Suzuki movies, characters' mental states are given visual

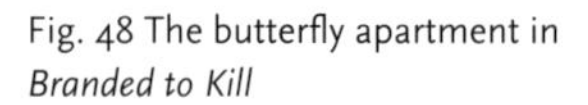

Fig. 48 The butterfly apartment in *Branded to Kill*

expression through the unorthodox use of color, lighting, and other visual effects, in *Branded* they actually dictate the mise-en-scene itself, infecting the film with their madness. The prime example is Misako's loony apartment decorated with butterflies, which is a visual projection of her mysterious eccentricities (fig. 48). Suzuki said that there is no fixed time and space in this film as opposed to in "normal" movies.[74] This gives an almost decadent freedom to the narrative. Unburdened by conventional motives, any character might do anything at any time. They are as abstract as humans can be. The city, too, is an abstraction, reduced to black-and-white patterns of straight lines, much cleaner in its geometry than the jumbled cityscapes of the earlier films. In his final Nikkatsu film, Suzuki's urge toward abstraction reaches its zenith.

"In My Films, Time and Place Are Nonsense"
Suzuki and the Aesthetics of the 1960s

Suzuki's artistic evolution in the 1960s involved an embrace of the nonsensical, a gradual dismantling of traditional cinematic narrative grammar. Critic David Chute described him as "a temperamental nihilist, perusing consciously the kind of startling, dislocated effects that can arise accidentally in transcendental bad movies, when the veil of illusion falls away."[75] This is what drew film students, and eventually astute film critics, to his work. Suzuki's violation of accepted cinematic codes and structures disrupts the suspension of disbelief that conventional films depend on, opening up new possibilities. The exaggerated acting performances and awkward effects that happen by chance in bad horror movies, for instance, become deliberate gestures, aimed at pointing out the essential artifice of film.

Suzuki didn't think of himself as an avant-garde artist; nor was he directly involved with the intertwined avant-garde scene and student protest movement of the 1960s. But his declaration in an interview that "it is necessary to destroy the traditional form and to go forward"[76] proves his intention to disrupt artistic convention, which he shared with artists across many disciplines at the time.

In Japan as in the United States during the 1960s, art, popular culture, and radical politics were arcing toward each other in a number of ways. Younger artists rejected refined forms in favor of an earthier, trashier aesthetic, part of which involved incorporating imagery from pop culture into their work. A 1965 painting by one of Japan's most prominent pop artists, Koichi Tateishi (aka Tiger Tateishi), called *Samurai, the Watcher* depicts a samurai overlooking a landscape that references American westerns, representing in "high art" the same conflation of American and Japanese cultural myths that Nikkatsu Action directors were pursuing. High art, pop culture imagery, and avant-garde aesthetics also united in the graphic designs of Yokoo Tadanori, the novels of Yukio Mishima, and the new form of dance popularly known as *butoh*.

Adventurous-minded and restless filmmakers were a key part of the trend. Film, music, dance, and visual art came together at the Sogetsu Art Center in Tokyo, a hub of cross-disciplinary avant-garde artistic practice in the 1960s. Artists, designers, dancers, performers, and filmmakers gathered to "test out new experimental practices and to engage in dialogue about new directions in the arts." There, "artists could collaborate and speak across disciplinary boundaries in ways that would have been impossible in traditional museum, concert hall, or academic contexts."[77]

Hiroshi Teshigahara, a filmmaker and ikebana flower arranger whose father founded the Sogetsu Art Center, ran the center himself from 1958 to 1971, presiding over this period of cross-disciplinary experimentation. It is a sign of just how much the worlds of avant-garde art and popular culture mixed during this time that Teshigahara would achieve mainstream success with films such as *Woman in the Dunes* (1964). Though it took an experimental approach to its narrative and visual design and featured a score by avant-garde composer Toru Takemitsu, the film played in mainstream theaters and was even nominated for two Academy Awards.

After honing their skills in the studio system, Shohei Imamura and Nagisa Oshima both struck out independently in the 1960s, seeking more creative freedom in subject matter and form, and mixing their studio-honed skills with experimental instincts. Imamura's landmark *A Man Vanishes* (1967) initially presents itself as a straightforward documentary about one of the many people who disappear from year to year in Japan before morphing into a radical questioning of the possibility of pursuing truth through cinema. Oshima's *Double Suicide: Japanese Summer* (1967) and *Death by Hanging* (1968) address controversial political issues (terrorism and the mistreatment of ethnic Koreans, respectively) using distancing techniques inspired by the work of Bertolt Brecht and Jean-Luc Godard. His *Three Resurrected Drunkards* (1968) challenges audience expectations by starting over in the middle and introducing subtle variations on what was already shown. (This movie is still so challenging that when I showed it a couple of years ago, people ran up to me in the back of the theater, convinced that the projectionist had mistakenly restarted the film from the beginning.)

These films are self-conscious: They call attention to their own construction by interrupting the illusion of narrative upon which commercial cinema depends, jarring viewers out of the narrative flow in order to remind them that they are watching a movie. *A Man Vanishes* points out that documentary films operate on their own set of accepted illusions, ones that Imamura systematically dismantles as the film progresses. *Death by Hanging* puts these techniques toward didactic ends. It blends narrative and documentary and addresses the viewer directly to inspire outrage over the story of a prisoner who, after a botched execution causes him to lose his memory, must be reminded of his crimes so that he can be executed again.

Donald Richie characterized Oshima as "a more serious Suzuki Seijun" who shares his "renegade inventiveness."[78] Indeed, Suzuki's self-consciousness in *Tokyo Drifter* and *Branded to Kill* is of a more playful variety. Both of these films poke fun at genre movie conventions by pushing them over the

Fig. 49 *Branded to Kill*

top and into parody. Their jagged editing rhythms, in which scenes sometimes seem to end in the middle of the action, jolt the viewer in and out of the story, emphasizing the arbitrariness of their plots. Their fight scenes, which dispense with logic in favor of spectacle and humor, underline the inherent silliness of the need for genre filmmakers to create ever more exciting action sequences. Gestures such as Tetsu in *Drifter* tossing a gun so he can dash across the room, catch it in mid-air, and shoot a bad guy—or when Hanada in *Branded* fires a bullet through a basement pipe (fig. 49) that emerges through a sink his target happens to be leaning over—can only be seen as jokes at the expense of the kinds of films Suzuki was supposed to be making.

This humorous, self-referential attitude would later be embraced by directors as varied as John Waters, Brian De Palma, and Sam Raimi, but during Suzuki's Nikkatsu years it was still quite avant-garde, more readily associated with Andy Warhol or George Kuchar than anyone working in the commercial film industry. Kuchar's campy *Hold Me While I'm Naked* (1966) assembles and disassembles the elements of Hollywood melodrama punctuated by scenes of Kuchar directing the very film we're watching. In Warhol's *Vinyl* (1965), his impassive, unmoving camera looks on as a pack of stoned Factory denizens slouch around, occasionally rousing themselves to act out scenes from *A Clockwork Orange*.

"In my films, time and place are nonsense," Suzuki once said.[79] This is especially true of *Tokyo Drifter* and *Branded to Kill*, which move from place to place and around in time with little motivation or explanation. With their embrace of nonsense and self-referential urge to expose the workings of the cinema machine, those two films most inspire commentators to grapple with Suzuki's avant-garde tendencies. Richard Scott called *Tokyo Drifter* a "dazzlingly stylish gangster movie that moves in the world of the 1960s, the Japanese counterpart to the explosion in graphics, fashion and music that in the west produced Warhol and Courreges, free-form psychedelia and op art's calculated precision, the sounds of the Beatles and the Beach Boys."[80] Daisuke Miyao argued that "*Branded* may be considered to be a self-referential modernist work made from within the Japanese studio system" and noted that Suzuki's values "have much in common with independent avant-garde filmmakers of the period."[81]

His films' absurdist comedy and anarchic energy also link them to the student protest movement. Tadao Sato saw Suzuki's sense of humor as allied with that of the counterculture, but pointed out that his acceptance of absurdity was even more ruthless. While the counterculture was clustered around a set of firmly held political ideals, "Suzuki was obsessed with the idea that all human endeavors are foolish, yet if one affirms this foolishness, it becomes all the more interesting. Thus, he sought meaning in the humor of mutability, and in his films humor replaced catharsis." Suzuki's willful, playful disruption of film form is an outgrowth of the freedom that accepting meaninglessness gave him, a conclusion he seems to have arrived at in parallel with many avant-garde artists of the time, even though he claims to be have been largely unaware of them.[82] The energies of restless B movie-makers, young artists, and radical students were all in the air at the time, creating a fertile environment for the kind of experimentation he embarked upon.

PLAYING WITH SURFACES: STYLE IN THE POST-NIKKATSU FILMS

Suzuki's 1960s experimentation stemmed in part from his confrontations with the limitations of the film medium and the inevitable two-dimensionality of the screen. The invisible floor in *Tattooed Life* is a remarkable visual device in its own right, but he also used actual glass floors in *Youth of the Beast* and *Tokyo Drifter* to form compositions that are off-kilter, angled, and fragmented, and that create a strong push-pull effect between the surface of the screen and the

Left: Fig. 50 A glass floor in *Youth of the Beast*

Right: Fig. 51 Dancers on a glass floor in *Tokyo Drifter*

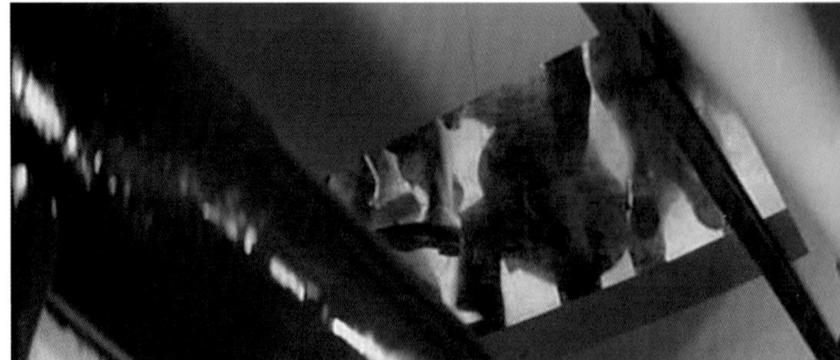

illusion of depth (fig. 50, fig. 51). Similarly, his theatrical choreography, sets, and lighting schemes tested the limitations of the cinematic illusion by collapsing it into theater (fig. 52), and the disjointed, nonsensical plots of his last two Nikkatsu films exploded the limitations of repetitive genre storylines.

Fig. 52 *Tattooed Life*

In his later films, freed from the demands of working for a commercial studio, Suzuki carried his experiments further. Along with the surface of the screen, surfaces and boundaries within it became porous borders between layers of reality or existential and spiritual realms. In some shots in *Yumeji* (1991), a film about a painter, the action takes place behind painted imagery, as if the scene were being viewed through a pane of glass (fig. 53).

Fig. 53 *Yumeji*

In a particularly complex sequence, even this illusion is broken. This scene presents a complex layering of narrative time through a succession of visual games. The characters sit facing frontally—though they are in dialogue with each other—behind blue raindrops, which, based on previous scenes, we assume to be painted on glass (fig. 54). They are discussing events surrounding a marriage that happened in the past, but one of them is wearing wedding attire, as if she is currently experiencing the events being recounted. She is framed by a

Fig. 54 *Yumeji*: What appear to be painted raindrops...

Fig. 55 ...are revealed to be solid when a keychain wraps around one of them.

window that visually isolates her from the other characters, as if it is also framing her in time, in a single-character flashback. But when a character throws a key on a chain, it loops around one of the "raindrops," revealing it to be solid (fig. 55). The thrown key, which is also part of the story being recounted, emerges from the past to destroy the glass illusion and create an even more perplexing one – that the raindrops are not painting, but sculpture. Within a single scene, Suzuki employed a sophisticated and entirely original interplay of visual surfaces in order to link different sequences of narrative time, all while emphasizing the permeability of time itself, which is a motif of his later films.

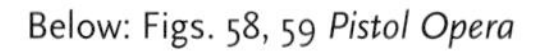

Like glass surfaces, mirrors were mainly used as playful formal devices in Suzuki's Nikkatsu films. They take on a mystical quality in the later ones. At one point, Yumeji looks into a mirror while holding a fan with his image drawn on it (fig. 56). In the next scene, he is attached by a rope to another man who is now holding the fan over his own face and claiming to be Yumeji (fig. 57). It's as if the mirror has literally reproduced him, and he is dragging this other self out into the world from beyond its surface.

Above: Figs. 56, 57 *Yumeji*

A mirror has the power to conjure reality in Suzuki's *Pistol Opera* (2001), which revisits the plot of *Branded to Kill*. A young girl, who in the film functions as a kind of ambassador or avatar of death for its assassin heroine (known as Stray Cat), paints on a mirror over the reflection of Stray Cat's face (fig. 58). When she's finished, the makeup has become real, and Stray Cat looks upon the reflection of her own perfectly made-up face (fig. 59).

Below: Figs. 58, 59 *Pistol Opera*

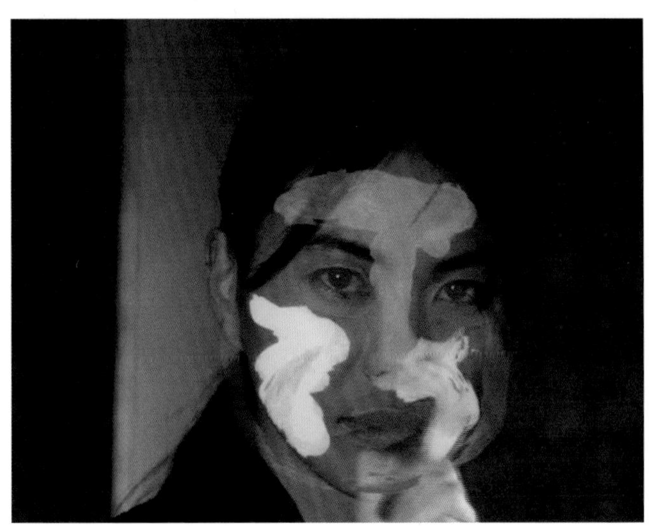

Fig. 60 *Pistol Opera*: the brick is removed to reveal...

Fig. 61 ...Painless Surgeon at his desk. Note yellow light.

Fig. 62 *Pistol Opera*: Painless Surgeon dies...

Fig. 63 ...and Stray Cat passes into a yellow room, where Painless Surgeon's desk now sits.

One battle with a rival assassin (called Painless Surgeon because he doesn't feel pain) is a complicated game of borders and symbols. As if presenting the scene to us, the young girl removes a brick from a wall (fig. 60), through which we see Painless Surgeon at his desk, on which sits a revolving yellow light (fig. 61). Yellow is the color of death in this film, so this light might be interpreted as a warning to him of its approach. After Stray Cat tricks him into stabbing himself (fig. 62), she walks into another space, lit completely in yellow, where his desk now mysteriously sits (fig. 63). The land of the dead has bled into the real world (if we can even call it that, since Painless Surgeon's office looks like a stage set). The planes of existence in this film are continually falling into one another in an infinite loop. It is no longer just the surface of the screen Suzuki is confronting, but the idea of surfaces and borders in general. It is an extension of the porous borders between life, death, waking, and dreaming that characterize the Taisho Trilogy of films he made in the 1980s and 1990s, in which not even the borderline of an edit is required to jump from the present to future.

Fig. 64 *Princess Raccoon*

In Suzuki's final and most good-natured film, *Princess Raccoon*, there is no attempt to knit its three distinct registers—CGI, theatrical sets, and the actual outdoors—into a seamless whole. Instead, each is emphasized as its own sort of illusion with its own surface. Suzuki poked fun once again at the idea of the screen as a window on reality when the film's hero and heroine sail against painted waves on a cutaway rowboat, as if the screen were slicing through it (fig. 64).

One way of looking at Suzuki's artistic evolution is to see it as a progression from testing limits to toying with them, and finally, to passing through them. For him, they are only illusions, after all. ●

29 Seijun Suzuki, "My Work," in *De woestijn onder de kersenbloesem—The Desert under the Cherry Blossoms* (Abcoude: Uitgeverij Uniepers, 1991), 31.

30 Seijun Suzuki and Koshi Ueno, "Forgetting Foreign Names," in *De woestijn onder de kersenbloesem—The Desert under the Cherry Blossoms* (Abcoude: Uitgeverij Uniepers, 1991), 67–68.

31 Ibid., 75.

32 Suzuki, "The Days of Kanto Mushuku," 39.

33 Suzuki and Ueno, "Forgetting Foreign Names," 68.

34 Suzuki, "The Days of Kanto Mushuku," 36.

35 Ibid., 38.

36 Hasumi, "A World without Seasons," 9.

37 Rayns, "The Kyoka Factor," 7.

38 Ibid., 6.

39 Schilling, *No Borders No Limits*, 9.

40 A handful of these films are now available online and in the Criterion Collection's *Eclipse Series 17: Nikkatsu Noir* DVD set.

41 Hasumi, "A World without Seasons," 18.

42 Seijun Suzuki, "Cinema, Film Directors and Oshima," in *De woestijn onder de kersenbloesem—The Desert under the Cherry Blossoms* (Abcoude: Uitgeverij Uniepers, 1991), 47.

43 Rayns, "The Kyoka Factor," 7.

44 A hallmark of Ozu's late style is the insertion of transitional shots that seem unrelated to the story and serve as a kind of punctuation between scenes. They came to be known as "pillow shots" for their cushioning effect.

45 Suzuki and Ueno, "Forgetting Foreign Names," 69.

46 In English-language credits, these words are usually reversed, but since it isn't actually a name, I will leave them in the original order.

47 Suzuki, "Suzuki on Suzuki," 25.

48 Stephen Teo, "Seijun Suzuki: Authority in Minority," *Senses of Cinema*, accessed April 20, 2015, http://sensesofcinema.com/2000/festival-reports/suzuki/

49 Ayako Uchida, interview with the author, Tokyo, July 27, 2013.

50 Suzuki, "Suzuki on Suzuki," 25.

51 Ibid., 25.

52 Hasumi, "A World without Seasons," 12.

53 Ibid., 9–10.

54 Seijun Suzuki et al., "The Tiger and the Messenger," in *De woestijn onder de kersenbloesem—The Desert under the Cherry Blossoms*, 73.

55 Hasumi, "A World without Seasons," 17.

56 Howard Hampton, "*Youth of the Beast*: Screaming Target," *The Criterion Collection*, accessed April 20, 2015, http://www.criterion.com/current/posts/351-youth-of-the-beast-screaming-target

57 Suzuki, "The Days of Kanto Mushuku," 33–40.

58 Seijun Suzuki, "Interview," *Youth of the Beast*, directed by Seijun Suzuki, 1963 (New York: The Criterion Collection, 2005), DVD.

59 Hasumi, "A World without Seasons," 18.

60 Suzuki, "Interview," *Youth of the Beast*.

61 Hasumi, "A World without Seasons," 22–23.

62 Takeo Kimura, "Interview," *Gate of Flesh*, directed by Seijun Suzuki, 1964 (New York: The Criterion Collection, 2005), DVD.

63 Ayako Uchida claims he just didn't give straight answers to interviewers he didn't like. Koshi Ueno says he never gives anyone a straight answer.

64 Kimura, "Interview," *Gate of Flesh*.

65 Suzuki, "Suzuki on Suzuki," 26–27.

66 Hasumi, "A World without Seasons," 15.

67 Seijun Suzuki, "The Desert under the Cherry Tree," in *De woestijn onder de kersenbloesem—The Desert under the Cherry Blossoms* (Abcoude: Uitgeverij Uniepers, 1991), 58.

68 Hasumi, "A World without Seasons," 11.

69 Suzuki, "Suzuki on Suzuki," 28.

70 Ibid., 29.

71 Schilling, *The Yakuza Movie Book*, 101.

72 Nikolaus Vyrzidis, "Tokyo Drifter," in *Directory of World Cinema: Japan* (Bristol: Intellect Books, 2010), 282.

73 Isolde Standish, *A New History of Japanese Cinema* (New York: The Continuum International Publishing Group, 2006), 309.

74 Seijun Suzuki, "Interview," *Branded to Kill*, directed by Seijun Suzuki, 1967 (New York: The Criterion Collection, 1999), DVD.

75 David Chute, "Branded to Thrill," *Branded to Thrill: The Delirious Cinema of Suzuki Seijun* (London: British Film Institute, 1995), 17.

76 Suzuki, Willemen, and Sato, *The Films of Seijun Suzuki*, 41.

77 Miki Kaneda, "A Very Brief History of the Sogetsu Art Center," accessed April 21, 2015, http://post.at.moma.org/content_items/154-a-very-brief-history-of-the-sogetsu-art-center

78 Richie, *A Hundred Years of Japanese Film*, 200.

79 Mes, "Japan Cult Cinema Interview: Seijun Suzuki."

80 Richard Scott, "Early Pop Guns," *The Times*, accessed April 21, 2015, http://sweetbottom.tripod.com/Articles/Oct151994.htm

81 Miyao, "Dark Visions," 201.

82 Or so he told me in response to an emailed query. Seijun Suzuki, email to the author (translated by Yuka Sakano), February 17, 2014.

4

SUZUKI'S COLLABORATIVE METHOD

COLLABORATING WITH CAST AND CREW

During his Nikkatsu career, Suzuki developed collaborative, improvisational working methods that involved surrounding himself with likeminded and talented technicians and encouraging their input. He would rely on these methods throughout his career. He has said that he wanted crew members to come to him with ideas and maintain a relaxed atmosphere on the set: "I wanted to lighten the mood. The director's job is to create an atmosphere that makes it easy for everyone to work." This approach extends to his treatment of actors. "I usually don't tell actors to do this or that," he said. "I let them do what they want. I only say something when they go off track."[83]

Suzuki has often claimed that he hated working at Nikkatsu, calling movie-making "painful work," and a "foolish, painful process,"[84] but he may have brought this on himself. According to Ayako Uchida, he would stay up all night making changes to scripts—which may account for his notorious habit of not bathing during shooting.

Uchida began working at the studio in 1964 as a script supervisor, one of the few crew positions available at the time to women in Hollywood or Japan. Called, in the old days, "script girls" or "continuity girls," their job included maintaining continuity between camera setups and noting any changes to the script made during shooting.[85] Though only in his early forties at the time, Suzuki was already known around the studio as "the old man," and friends recommended that Uchida try to work for him because of his reputation for treating his crews well.[86]

She recalled that Suzuki frequently eschewed the director's chair and sat on the ground amongst his underlings during his Nikkatsu years, an almost unheard-of violation of the hierarchical nature of film crews at the time. In

Opposite: *Underworld Beauty*. See page 79.

behind-the-scenes footage of 2005's *Princess Raccoon*, he can even be seen kneeling on the studio floor to direct scenes, at an age when he had every right to work from a comfortable perch. Uchida also remembered being shocked when, early in her career, he asked her—one of the lowest-ranking crew members—for input on how a scene should be shot.

According to Shigehiko Hasumi, as Suzuki's career went on:

> Young assistant directors started to compete fiercely for a position on his crew. In their enthusiasm, they offered him ideas for the tiniest details. Before long, they formed a new group of anonymous screenwriters. The key figure of the group was Yamatoya Atsushi, who would later make a number of interesting films as an independent director. The group, consisting of eight people and called *Guryu Hachiro* ("Group of Eight"), acted like a secret society devoted to Suzuki Seijun, and this led to envy among the studios' other assistant directors.[87]

The *Guryu Hachiro* group, which included Suzuki himself, would eventually be credited with the screenplay for *Branded to Kill*. Hasumi saw this group as enabling the rebelliousness that would lead to the showdown between Suzuki and his studio bosses over that film.

Throughout his career, Suzuki has remained fiercely loyal to collaborators who understand him. Uchida went on to work for him on several films at Nikkatsu as well as all of his later films (with the exception of *A Tale of Sorrow and Sadness*). Yamatoya worked on the screenplays for *A Tale of Sorrow and Sadness* (1977), *Capone Cries A Lot*, and the anime *Lupin III: Legend of the Gold of Babylon* (both 1985). As we've seen, at Nikkatsu, Suzuki also worked closely with the cinematographers Shigeyoshi Mine and Kazue Nagatsuka, and, perhaps most importantly, the art director Takeo Kimura. He too worked with Suzuki all the way through *Princess Raccoon*.

Hasumi noted that, at Nikkatsu, Suzuki "was a craftsman first. ... He needed only a regular, well-trained and experienced crew to realize his ideas within the studio system." With Kimura, Nagatsuka, and Mine, he assembled "the perfect team as far as photography and art direction were concerned. ... The typical visual games he developed during this period were the result of lengthy deliberation with his camera man and his art director."[88]

Suzuki gave a glimpse of Mine and Kimura's personalities, and how their collaboration worked at its height, by describing a night of drinking with them while shooting *Tokyo Drifter*:

> Kimura has confidence in Mine's talent, with whom he is able to create an image like a *sumi-e* [a traditional ink-wash painting]. But the characters of the two men do not harmonize well. Mine is impulsive, Kimura is complex. One trait they have in common is that they are both egotists. ... When they are drinking sake, their ego emerges with greater force. ...They discuss the photography of [*Tokyo Drifter*], in which the snow is the protagonist of the story. I'm being canny. I wait until they stop arguing. Sometimes they turn to me, but I don't respond, because for me it is enough to decide at the time when the camera has to be set up. The snow already has provoked something in these men, whichever image of the snow will eventually transpire.

Working with assigned scripts on tight deadlines, Suzuki was forced to adjust his methods to his working conditions. The rapport he established with his key collaborators enabled them to work creatively and quickly. As he told Schilling, "From the time I got the script until shooting I had about one or two weeks. ... No-name directors like me had zero time, so I had no choice

"I was just trying to grind out program pictures. I wasn't trying to stand out from anyone else. ...When I thought about making the film more interesting and suspenseful, it was all for the audience. I was there to serve them."

but to stay up all night and never go home." All that late-night work—not to mention the strategic yet sociable drinking sessions with his crew—was, for him, in the service of making the scripts he was given more interesting for the audience, not for creating a signature style: "I was just trying to grind out program pictures. I wasn't trying to stand out from anyone else. ...When I thought about making the film more interesting and suspenseful, it was all for the audience. I was there to serve them."[89]

The collaborative method he developed to achieve these goals extends beyond how he worked with his crew to the way he reacted to the actors, settings, and materials at his disposal. Suzuki characterized his method for directing actresses as focusing on their most attractive aspect (which could be as specific as hands or even fingers) and finding their individuality through the way they moved their bodies.[90] This is clear even in *Underworld Beauty*, made five years before the 1963 run of films in which his distinct style began to make itself known. The film seems to sag whenever its star, the energetic Mari Shiraki, isn't onscreen, throwing herself around in the throes of extreme emotions (there are no subtle ones). Shiraki's energy drives the film, and this is a key to Suzuki's technique—encouraging spontaneity in both his actors and himself. He considers storyboards "boring" and believes that "improvisation makes the picture."[91] He urged his actors to improvise in reaction to costumes, sets, and the overnight script changes he would spring on them. Even when cast in minor roles in Suzuki's films (such as her role as a bargirl in *The Sleeping Beast Within* or as a withdrawing heroin addict in *Passport to Darkness*), Shiraki distinguishes her scenes from the rest of the film because of Suzuki's willingness to give her exuberance free rein.

It isn't just actresses that inspired this give-and-take. Films such as *Gate of Flesh* and *Branded to Kill* derive much of their manic energy from Jo Shishido's bull-in-a-china-shop performances. It's no accident that Suzuki's stylistic breakthrough came with *Youth of the Beast*, in which Shishido manages to even take a shower violently, and, according to Suzuki, came up with the idea of conducting a gunfight while hanging upside down.[92] In these films, you can see Suzuki feeding off of and encouraging Shishido's outrageousness in ways other directors didn't. The actor's performance in Nomura's *A Colt is My Passport*, for instance, is markedly more restrained than anything he did for Suzuki—as is, for that matter, Shiraki's performance in Masuda's *Rusty Knife*.

He urged his actors to improvise in reaction to costumes, sets, and the overnight script changes he would spring on them.

Energetic physicality is key to Shishido's performances. The same is true of the performances Suzuki elicited from his preferred actresses. "Perhaps Suzuki refuses to recognize the difference between men and women," suggested Shigehiko Hasumi. "His favourite actors use a physical approach, not a psychological one, to flesh out their roles." I wouldn't go so far as to say that Suzuki sees no difference between men and women, but the actresses in his Nikkatsu films do tend to exhibit a tough, noisy energy that he makes no attempt to soften or feminize. Yumiko Nogawa, for example, starred as a prostitute in Suzuki's *Gate of Flesh*, *Story of a Prostitute*, and *Carmen from Kawachi*. Her character is a "robust woman who manages to hold her own in a world populated by gangsters, yakuza and schoolboys acting tough. Her most appealing moments are not those when she seems to lose herself in her love for a man, but when Suzuki gives her restrained sensuality a certain fierceness."[93] Her most memorable moments in these films are those involving fortitude or action, as when she throws a sexual predator over a waterfall in *Carmen*, exhibits the stoicism of a hardened yakuza after being whipped in *Gate of Flesh*, or runs across a battlefield to save a wounded soldier in *Prostitute* (fig. 65). In these scenes, Nogawa is no less an action star than Jo Shishido or Akira Kobayashi. As with Mari Shiraki in *Underworld Beauty*, these films' energy and pacing come from Suzuki reacting to Nogawa's specific physicality and vitality.

When saddled with lackluster performers, Suzuki had to be responsive in a different way. While directing Tatsuya Watari in *Tokyo Drifter*, Suzuki and Kimura went to absurd lengths with surreal sets, lurid colors, and bizarre staging to compensate for Watari's wooden screen presence. Although Watari

Fig. 65 Yumiko Nogawa in *Story of a Prostitute*

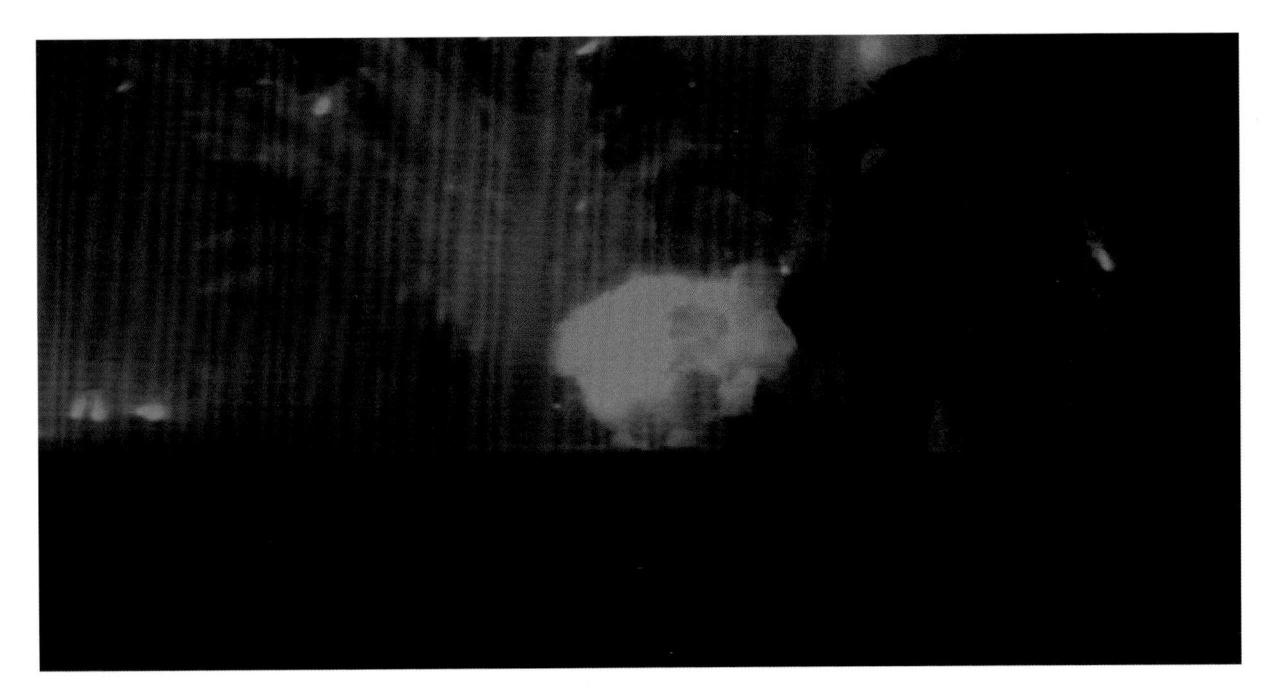

was an established star at the time, Suzuki claimed that he would freeze when Suzuki called "action" and had to be physically prodded by an assistant to say his lines.[94]

Only in Suzuki's final film, *Princess Raccoon*, does this technique of either reacting to or overcompensating for acting performances fall flat. Its capable (and, in other films, compelling) stars Zhang Ziyi and Jo Odagiri at times just seem to be hitting their marks. But in that case, Suzuki's job was made harder by the relatively new technology of CGI. This required his actors to play many scenes against a green screen, with little or no set decoration to react to, and could account for their at times blank and glassy-eyed expressions.

The uneven performances in *Princess Raccoon* can be forgiven considering that Suzuki was in his eighties and lacking the energy he once had. In interviews from the 1990s and 2000s, he often made a point of how physically punishing filmmaking is. But *Princess Raccoon*'s flaws could also be attributable to his habit of letting actors used to a firm directorial hand chart their own course. One of the conclusions his script supervisor Uchida came to after working with him for so many years was that his deference to crew members and actors had its downside. She said she felt that he was as reluctant to criticize as he was eager to seek input.[95]

REACTING TO SETTINGS

Just as Suzuki encouraged his actors to improvise, he reacted to settings when directing scenes. This is most apparent in the films he made before he and Kimura started creating deliberately perverse visual worlds in the studio, as well as in his films shot in places where that kind of manipulation wasn't possible. He fed off the energy of machines in the opening motorcycle chase in *Naked Age* (aka *Age of Innocence,* 1959), which surges with engine noise and speed, much like he fed off of Shiraki's energy in *Underworld Beauty.* When

The outdoor, open spaces where these scenes take place seem to have energized Suzuki, but he couldn't seem to find similar inspiration in the indoor spaces where most of the film is set.

a gang of friends takes a road trip to a beach resort in his juvenile delinquent drama *Everything Goes Wrong* (1960), the film surges with the kinetic energy sparked by their joyride in a careening sports car. The outdoor, open spaces where these scenes take place seem to have energized Suzuki, but he couldn't seem to find similar inspiration in the indoor spaces where most of the film is set. Filmed head-on and with little camera movement, these interior scenes feel distinctly inert compared to the outdoor ones.

Urban settings also energize this born and bred Tokyoite's work much more than rural ones. In the noir caper *Take Aim at the Police Van!,* he made creative use of Tokyo's jumbled geography in two chase scenes that involve cars and trains in parallel but separate planes of action. The film noir atmosphere of the kidnapping thriller *Passport to Darkness* gave him license to play with extremes of light and dark when evoking a dangerous, seedy, nocturnal Tokyo. *Smashing the O-Line* (1960), a caper about drug dealers and double crosses, conveys a restless energy as its protagonist, an unapologetically amoral, nihilist reporter who will betray anyone to get a story, makes his way through its bustling urban locations.

That energy is lacking entirely in *The Blood-Red Channel*, made a year later and set in a fishing village on a small island. Another director might have emphasized the natural beauty of the seaside setting, but Suzuki didn't take advantage of it. (It didn't help that he was saddled with an especially clichéd script about two brothers, one a coast guard member and the other a smuggler, who come into predictable conflict.) It's as if the tranquility of the setting gave him nothing to react against. The rugged, mountainous landscapes of *The Man with a Shotgun*, on the other hand, inspired visual ideas for staging action scenes among boulders, tall trees, and a precarious bridge across a river. With its references to the Old West, the script also gave him more to work with, providing ample opportunity to play with cowboy movie tropes in surroundings that suited them.

When Suzuki did shoot on a soundstage, he often didn't have much of a budget to dress the sets. Some of the most memorable visual ideas from his post-1963 period—the colorful dresses popping against dull backgrounds in *Gate of Flesh* or the minimalist nightclub with a bizarre donut-shaped sculpture in *Tokyo Drifter*, for example—are the result of Suzuki and Kimura improvising creatively with limited means. They enthusiastically dispensed with realism in order to create visuals that were striking in their own right.

Suzuki is a specialist in improving run-of-the-mill material by putting his stylistic stamp on it, but sometimes even he couldn't fix a bad script.

Suzuki is a specialist in improving run-of-the-mill material by putting his stylistic stamp on it, but sometimes even he couldn't fix a bad script. Though it was made in the midst of the mid-1960s creative surge, we can see him spin his wheels in *Born under Crossed Stars* (1965), a cliché-riddled story about a righteous young man torn between a good girl and a bad girl. Uchida told me that Suzuki once asked an assistant director to bring a monkey to the set the next day, which puzzled Uchida because there was no monkey in the script.[96] It transpired that he wanted it for a single throwaway joke: After the film's hero, who sells milk door-to-door, tries to convince a customer to buy some (lest her child end up malnourished and looking "like a monkey"), Suzuki cut to a brief shot of the monkey he ordered, in a carriage swaddled in baby clothes. It's a long way to go for a corny gag. A similar, if more amusing, moment happens later on when the camera pans along a group of couples necking in a park with exaggerated smooching noises on the soundtrack. It's almost as if he was trying to make the script's already corny humor even more groan-inducing through exaggeration.

OZU'S SHADOW

In his improvisational methods, Suzuki couldn't be more different from Yasujiro Ozu. The most famous director at Shochiku, where Suzuki served his apprenticeship, Ozu sought to control every aspect of his films. Suzuki's method may even have been a reaction against what Ozu represented. After work, Suzuki and his fellow assistant directors would get together to drink and plot the overthrow of Ozu, Mizoguchi, and Kurosawa, the titans of the day. Along with other members of his generation, such as Oshima and

Fig. 66 Setsuko Hara in Yasujiro Ozu's *Late Spring*

Imamura (who worked as Ozu's assistant and was famous for his laziness), Suzuki set out to upend the tasteful classicism represented by their mentors. Oshima articulated their rebellious attitude when he said in an interview that Ozu and Mizoguchi's films "were made to be acceptable to the Japanese because they were based upon a familiar set of general concepts readily understandable by the Japanese—they used a narrative style long established and understood, but I am not attempting to remain within this congenial, older mode."[97]

Ozu's shadow still loomed over Suzuki as late as 1986. In a discussion of *Zigeunerweisen*, part of the Taisho Trilogy, Koshi Ueno asked Suzuki if he thought he had been "unkind" to leave so much unexplained in that film. Suzuki responded by comparing his methods to Ozu's:

> At Shochiku you had Ozu, for instance; he was very orderly. Someone enters at the back of a corridor, calls out: "I'm home," opens the door and takes off his shoes. Ozu never starts in the middle of a scene, the way I do. That's his method.[98]

It's hard to imagine two more different stylists working within the same commercial film industry in such experimental ways: Ozu, the rigorous structuralist, and Suzuki, the freewheeling anarchist. Ozu's minimalism and precision were the result of his notoriously controlling methods. He

Fig. 67 Mari Shiraki in *Underworld Beauty*

rehearsed his actors until their line deliveries were drained of any personal expression and carefully composed his shots for subtle formal and dramatic effects. This is why no other films look or feel quite like those of his mature postwar style, which he honed to such a fine point that they resemble variations on a theme, their dramatic impact made even more powerful by the minimalism of their structure. In these rigorously controlled spaces, even the subtlest of facial expressions takes on a devastating power. In this sense, Setsuko Hara is perhaps the quintessential Ozu actress, able to convey depths of pain with a slight turn of her head or a tiny droop in her nearly ever-present smile (fig. 66).

Contrast this with Mari Shiraki's wildcat performance in *Underworld Beauty* (1957), the first film Suzuki made under his assumed *nom de cinema*. A year after Hara quietly illuminated Ozu's *Tokyo Twilight*, Shiraki ping-ponged through Suzuki's gangster potboiler with a ferocious sexual energy, playing a reckless hedonist in constant search of pleasure or oblivion (fig. 67).

Developed partly out of necessity, Suzuki's collaborative method was also the result of his temperament and personality. He recognized and encouraged his collaborators' particular talents and was modest enough to defer to their expertise. In return, he received their loyalty and benefited greatly from their unique contributions. Suzuki's burst of creativity from 1963 on would be unthinkable without the input of the likes of Kimura and Shishido. Recognizing and incorporating their talents into his films is a talent in itself. ●

83 Schilling, *The Yakuza Movie Book*, 99.

84 Ibid., 226.

85 The job still exists today, but without the sexist name.

86 Ayako Uchida, interview.

87 Hasumi, "A World without Seasons," 20.

88 Ibid., 13–14.

89 Schilling, *The Yakuza Movie Book*, 99.

90 Seijun Suzuki, "Interview," *Story of a Prostitute*, directed by Seijun Suzuki, 1965 (New York: The Criterion Collection, 2005), DVD.

91 Seijun Suzuki, "Interview," *Tokyo Drifter*, directed by Seijun Suzuki, 1966 (New York: The Criterion Collection, 1999), DVD.

92 Seijun Suzuki, "Interview," *Youth of the Beast*.

93 Hasumi, "A World without Seasons," 20–21.

94 Suzuki, "Interview," *Tokyo Drifter*.

95 Uchida, interview.

96 Ibid.

97 Richie, *A Hundred Years of Japanese Film*, 197–98.

98 Suzuki and Ueno, "Forgetting Foreign Names," 74.

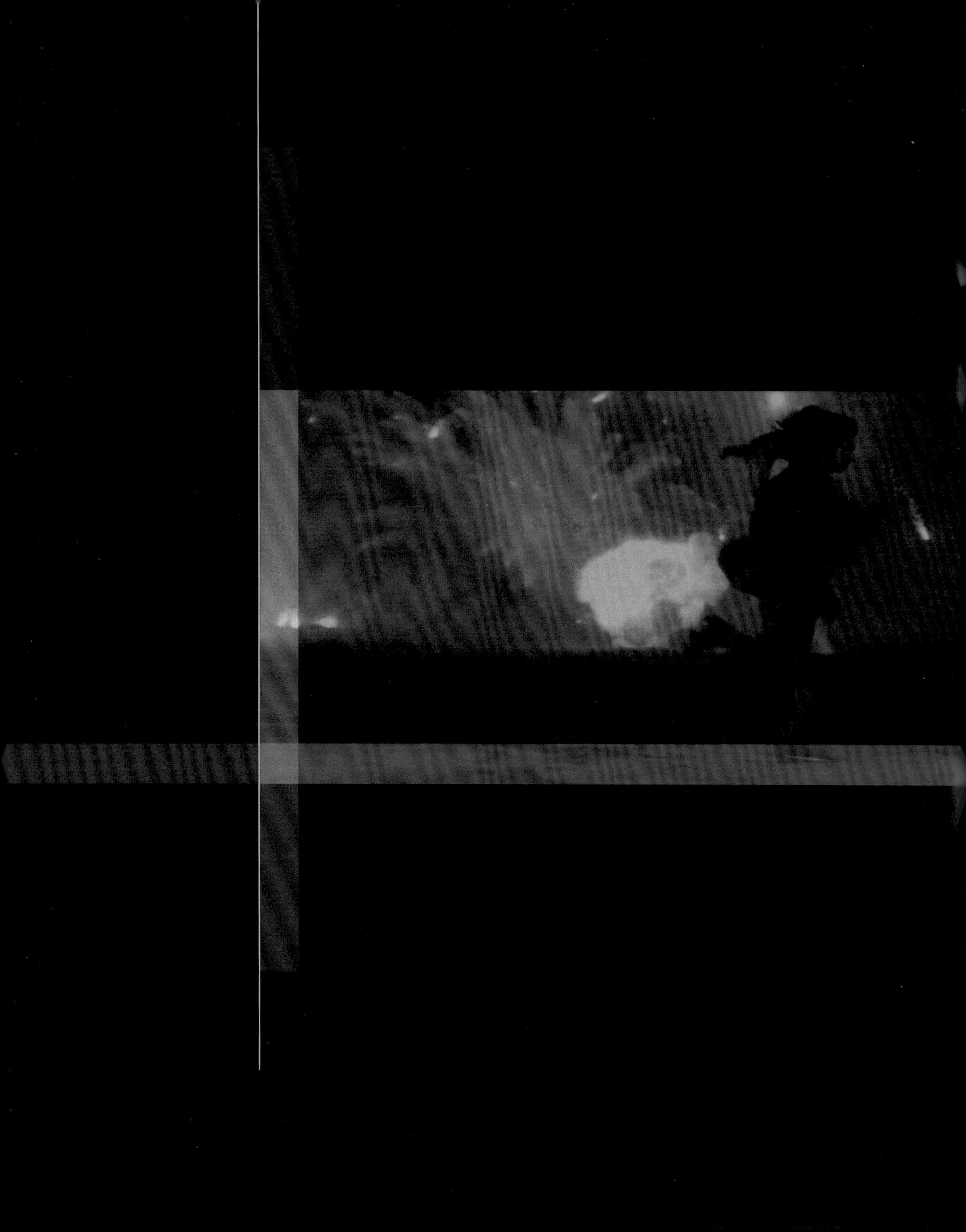

5

WAR AND NIHILISM, SEX AND VIOLENCE

SUZUKI'S WARTIME EXPERIENCES

In 1943, Suzuki was drafted into the Imperial Japanese Army as part of the national student mobilization effort, serving in the Philippines and Taiwan until the end of the war and achieving the rank of private second class. Two of the transport ships he traveled on were sunk by American forces. In one case, he spent more than seven hours in the water waiting to be rescued. In "My Work," a 1972 essay he wrote about his time in the army and his early film career, he wrote that during his time in the army he "spent most of my money on booze and women, and when I arrived at Tanabe harbor the year after liberation, I was completely destitute."[99]

Suzuki's wartime experience imbued him with a nihilist, absurdist attitude toward the world that appears, subtly and overtly, throughout his Nikkatsu career. "War," he wrote, "turns individual wishes and behaviour into something utterly ridiculous. War is simply praying 'don't let me die.'"[100]

This attitude also came out in interviews about his wartime experiences, in which he seemed to relish shocking his interlocutors by turning the harrowing events he experienced into comedy. In one interview, he said, "But war is funny, you know! When you're in the middle of it, you can't help laughing. ... I was thrown into the sea during a bombing raid. As I was drifting, I got the giggles."[101] In another, he described the sight of shipwreck victims being hoisted onto the deck of a ship by a rope, bouncing against it all the way up until they "had lumps all over their bodies, and they looked so funny." He went on to describe a burial at sea in which ten bodies were thrown overboard, one after the other, accompanied by a bugle fanfare: "Each time we heard the sound of the bugle, it was followed by that of the body plunking in the water. The tata-tata of the bugle and the plunking sound didn't go together at all. It was really funny."[102]

Opposite: *Story of a Prostitute*

NIHILISM AS AN AFFIRMATION OF LIFE

Nihilism was a natural reaction to, or mental defense against, the devastation that World War II brought to Japan. Many directors were similarly affected, and some expressed it in darker ways than Suzuki did. In Yasuzo Masumura's *Red Angel* (1966), a doctor serving at the front during the Sino-Japanese War has seen so much carnage that he ceases to believe in anything, preferring instead to numb himself with morphine to the point of impotence. Of the many films portraying the nihilistic postwar generation, Nagisa Oshima's *Cruel Story of Youth* (1960) is perhaps the most powerful. In it, a desperately cynical young character declares that he and his generation "have no dreams, so we won't see them destroyed."

Suzuki, on the other hand, managed to turn nihilism into a life-affirming credo, albeit one rooted in a belief that life is fundamentally absurd. Asked by an interviewer if he thought that "war is funny due to the thought that everything is temporary," Suzuki responded: "That's part of it, yes. But to be honest, it's probably sentimentality. Life is finite, man is bound to die." He then drew a parallel between the insanity of war and that of his revenge-obsessed yakuza characters: "I think they're related somehow. Yakuza are also destined to die, and that is absurd. They are aware of the absurdity from the start, but they bear their destiny honestly. There's something tragic about that."[103]

His writings and interviews give the impression of a guy disinclined to take anything seriously, least of all himself. Here, for example, is how he began "My Work":

> It seems there are only two kinds of people: people with only pleasant memories and people with only bad memories. They both have good memories. It's hard to determine which is the happier kind, but in general people with only pleasant memories will be more enviable than people with only bad and painful memories, because they are undoubtedly an important aid in developing a strong personality.
>
> On the other hand, there are idiots who have no memories at all. There is a man whose memory is so bad that he can't remember the name of the film he saw yesterday, or completely forgets the name or face of the person he has seen for the first time today, and he has just left. I am that man. So it's very exhausting for me to remember all sorts of things about my work, or about what happened to me a quarter of a century ago, whether they are pleasant memories or not. For a forgetful person such as I, work, just like infatuation, love, living together, getting married and dying is no more than a

> gust of wind blowing past your head. When it's over, it's forgotten right away. That's why you shouldn't expect the following story to be completely true. Not just because I am a forgetful liar, but because everything in this world consists of fifty percent lies and fifty percent truth.[104]

Tadao Sato suggested that Suzuki possesses a nihilism "so extreme it becomes an affirmation of life."[105] Just twenty years old when he went to war, Suzuki was of a generation that came of age knowing nothing but militarism. Filmmakers from the generation preceding his, such as Kurosawa and Keisuke Kinoshita, "had received a Marxist baptism in their youth," instilling in them a sense of social justice and sympathy for the underdog that comes

---

Suzuki, on the other hand, managed to turn nihilism into a life-affirming credo, albeit one rooted in a belief that life is fundamentally absurd.

through in their work. Oshima and other members of the generation following Suzuki's saw firsthand the shortcomings of several schools of thought: militarism leading the country into a disastrous war, Marxism degenerating into Stalinism. This instilled in them an attitude of "opposition to oppression in any form."[106]

Sato argued that the most influential ideology for young intellectuals of Suzuki's generation was Hideo Kobayashi's concept of evanescence (*mujokan*). "By stressing the mutability of all things," wrote Sato, "he made young, intelligent men accept death and destruction on the battlefield." An influential literary critic and public intellectual, Kobayashi was a fervent wartime propagandist, asserting that it was fruitless to question the validity or reasons for wars as they are beyond human reason or control. All that mattered was duty to the emperor who declared them. After the war, Kobayashi considered Japan's defeat "merely a continuation of mutability, and he thought people should forget the horrors and sufferings and simply adjust to the present."

The mutability Suzuki witnessed firsthand during the war was of a decidedly less theoretical nature: that of bodies torn apart by weaponry. Having grown up immersed in the ideas that Kobayashi and others promulgated, and having experienced the destructive nature of war first-hand, he came to accept that destruction was the motivating power in the world. He found it hard to believe that a society so completely indoctrinated into an ideology of conquest and destruction could suddenly about-face and pour the same fervor into democracy and peaceful reconstruction. The will to destroy was, in his opinion, not so easy to cast aside. "I think what remains in our memory is not 'construction' but 'destruction,'" he said in an interview in 1969. "Making things is not what counts. The power that destroys them is."

The war turned him into a fatalist, and his fatalism wouldn't allow him to throw his lot in with the likes of Oshima and the student activists of the 1960s: Their ideology, as laudable as it was, could easily degenerate into something ugly, and often it did. Koji Wakamatsu, himself a veteran of radical politics in Japan in the 1960s, treated the matter quite movingly in his elegiac 2007 film *United Red Army*, based on his own experiences in Japan's radical underground. The film follows a group of 1960s student protestors who morph into terrorists as their idealism curdles into dogma, and their leaders' motives revert to the violent, destructive impulses that postwar reconstruction was supposed to have replaced. "Power exists, too," Suzuki said in the 1969

It is an extreme expression of wariness about mass movements in the 1960s that Suzuki shared with other artists.

interview. "But we don't have to put on a red helmet [like the student activists] to resist it. I'm saying it's better to do nothing at all."[107]

This may sound like a shockingly apathetic position, but it makes a certain amount of sense coming from someone who at the time was being held up as a counterculture hero simply for making movies. It is an extreme expression of wariness about mass movements in the 1960s that Suzuki shared with other artists. (It reminds me of Frank Zappa's response to an audience member who objected to the officers keeping order at a concert in the late 1960s: "Everybody in this room is wearing a uniform, and don't kid yourself."[108]) Years ago, when I interviewed the American filmmaker Jon Jost for a tiny film zine, he told me he could never join the mass protests in the 1960s, despite being at least as far left on the political spectrum as the protesters. He got the impression that most members of the movement were just looking for someone to tell them what to think, and the people on the left happened to be the most convincing.

But such quotes are also part of Suzuki's perverse pattern of elusiveness and self-contradiction in interviews, which is in line with his commitment to taking nothing seriously. This is the good-natured part of his nihilism. His profound disillusionment led him to embrace the absurd, and absurd humor pervades even—and perhaps especially—his most violent films. As Sato put it, "Suzuki's best films take on the semblance of a masochistic cartoon."[109]

SEX AND VIOLENCE

I was a little surprised to see Paul Willemen, in an essay for a Suzuki retrospective at the 1988 Edinburgh Film Festival, go to great pains to prepare the audience for what he called "the most disturbing aspects of his work, for non-Japanese viewers," namely, "his deployment of violence and eroticism, particularly when these two taboos occur in combination." He warned potential viewers away who find the films of Samuel Fuller or Sam Peckinpah too violent,[110] and even went so far as to include a lengthy quote from an Ian Buruma book explaining the phenomenon of violent imagery in Japanese pop culture.

Maybe I'm jaded, but I would never think of issuing a similar warning today. I suppose it's partly because, as with many things that seemed shocking in their day, the violence in Suzuki's films is quite tame by today's standards, and he staged his scenes in such a way as to deliberately distance us from any sense of reality. When there is blood, it is of the gooey, bright red, prop blood variety, used as much for its aesthetic qualities as to depict injury. In *Tokyo Drifter*, for instance, we realize a character has been shot when she falls to the floor and a tiny, perfect pearl of bright red blood appears on her chest.

Because he designed his fight scenes as spectacles, the impressions they leave are of their choreography and visual design. The reddening ground, quick tracking shots, and sliding shoji screens in the final battle in *Tattooed Life*, and the shoji screens falling away to a red screen followed by an abrupt cut to a snowy landscape during the finale of *Kanto Wanderer*, are two striking examples. Other violent scenes are intentionally pitched toward humor and camp, as when Jo Shishido conducts a gunfight while hanging upside down in *Youth of the Beast* or virtually any fight scene in *Tokyo Drifter* or *Branded to Kill*, especially *Drifter*'s barroom brawl, which is presented as pure slapstick comedy.

Even the rape and torture scenes in *Youth of the Beast* and *Gate of Flesh* have such an artificial quality that they aren't nearly as disturbing as the many rape and torture scenes in Japanese "pink films" or as creepy as the smirking voyeurism of American "sexploitation" films. The latter films do not become quaint, to me, for being old, because the impulses behind them are less benign than Suzuki's were. Even though Suzuki's habit of portraying prostitutes and bargirls as independent and sassy is a cliché in itself, it's a far less harmful one than presenting them as objects to be ogled or violated. In fact, it seems to stem from the "first-hand experience" he had with prostitutes during the war.[111]

Other directors also looked for ways to portray the new postwar reality in more truthful, forceful ways than the classical tradition could offer. Working in B movies, a genre in which violence was an acceptable form of expression, gave them freedom to do so. Kinji Fukasaku, another director who pulled at the seams of genre aesthetics, survived an artillery attack on the munitions factory where he worked as a teenager during the war. After the war, he found himself "surrounded by piles of charred rubble and black markets. I wanted to make films for the young people who were having to live, wounded and bleeding. I think that's the reason I was so into crime films."[112] Many student protesters "thought the yakuza film characters were almost like the student leaders, fighting the system against impossible odds."[113] *Red Angel* director Masumura, who, like Suzuki, saw combat during the war, developed a similarly flamboyant style, trading on violence and eroticism, and often savagely parodying postwar cultural trends. His 1958 film *Giants and Toys*, for instance, satirized Japan's new consumerism, corporate culture, and worship of media stars by portraying the ruthless competition between two candy companies. As with Suzuki's work, in Masumura's films "eroticism and cruelty would often go hand in hand."[114]

Perhaps Willemen chose to warn his audience about Suzuki's films because, in 1988, mainstream movies generally were less violent than they are today. Of the many reasons for this, one is that the filmmakers—such as Quentin Tarantino—had not yet discovered the work of directors such as Suzuki and popularized such stylized sex and violence through their own films. The difference between Suzuki and his contemporaries' use of violence and that of Tarantino and his peers is a matter of intent. Suzuki used B movie potboilers such as *Story of a Prostitute* and *Gate of Flesh* as vehicles for condemning Japanese and American imperialism. Tarantino, in my opinion, used the horrors of World War II and slavery as excuses to make joke-filled action movies in *Inglourious Basterds* (2009) and *Django Unchained* (2013).[115]

An interesting study could be done comparing the violence in films by directors who actually experienced it, such as Suzuki, Fuller, and Fukasaku, and those whose experience of violence comes only from seeing it in movies. One reason for the stylized, cartoon-like violence in Suzuki's work may be that, having seen the real thing, he had no desire to inflict it on an audience. ●

99 Suzuki, "My Work," 29.

100 Seijun Suzuki, "Random Notes on Fellini (or: I don't like it)," *De woestijn onder de kersenbloesem—The Desert under the Cherry Blossoms* (Abcoude: Uitgeverij Uniepers, 1991), 52.

101 Suzuki et al., "The Tiger and the Messenger," 62–66.

102 Sato, *Currents in Japanese Cinema*, 225.

103 Suzuki et al., "The Tiger and the Messenger," 63.

104 Suzuki, "My Work," 27.

105 Tadao Sato, "Interview," *Story of a Prostitute.*

106 Sato, *Currents in Japanese Cinema*, 223.

107 Ibid., 224.

108 Frank Zappa, vocal performance of "Little House I Used to Live In," by Frank Zappa, recorded 1967–69, on Frank Zappa and the Mothers, *Burnt Weeny Sandwich*, Zappa Records, audio CD.

109 Sato, *Currents in Japanese Cinema*, 225.

110 Suzuki, Willemen, and Sato, *The Films of Seijun Suzuki*, 33.

111 Suzuki, "Interview," *Story of a Prostitute.*

112 Chris Desjardins, *Outlaw Masters of Japanese Film* (London: I.B. Tauris & Co. Ltd., 2005), 113.

113 Ibid., 82.

114 Tom Mes, "Yasuzo Masumura: Passion and Excess," accessed April 21, 2015, http://www.midnighteye.com/features/yasuzo-masumura-passion-and-excess/

115 I happen to enjoy both of these movies on a visceral level even as they make me uncomfortable on an intellectual one.

6

SUZUKI'S WAR FILMS

Despite Suzuki's disavowal of seriousness, there is a solemn critique of militarist ideology and structures of authority running through the three films he made about war and its aftermath: *Fighting Elegy*, *Story of a Prostitute*, and *Gate of Flesh*. There is a passion behind them that is not seen in films on lighter subjects, such as *The Call of Blood* and *Born under Crossed Stars*, that he made around the same time, and they exemplify Donald Richie's contention that, in many Suzuki films, "amid all the blood and laughter, a serious point is being made."[116] *Elegy*, *Prostitute*, and *Gate* expose the links between sexual repression and militarized violence, and present explicit condemnations of both Japanese and American imperialism. As Stephen Teo put it:

> *Story of a Prostitute* and *Fighting Elegy* are melodramas of Japanese militarism, studded with hysterical and hilarious depictions of the rise of Japanese fascism through the educational establishment and the army, and the ideology's subjugation and distortion of sexual desire in its push to gain hegemony over the whole of East Asia. As studies of Japanese militarism or the militaristic mind-set that was the cause of so much pain and suffering, these two films remain in a class of their own, quite unequalled by other Japanese films that I have seen.[117]

FIGHTING ELEGY

Fighting Elegy stars Hideki Takahashi as Kiroku, a teenager staying with another family while he attends high school. He develops a crush on the devoutly Catholic daughter and finds that the only way he can release his unbearable sexual tension is to get into fights. When that isn't enough, he starts rebelling against his teachers and is sent to another school, where he

Opposite: *Gate of Flesh*. See page 95.

organizes students into a gang to fight kids from a rival school. By the end of the film, Kiroku's sexual energy has been turned in an altogether more dangerous direction as he sets off to join the fight in the Sino-Japanese War.

There are slapstick moments throughout the film, as when Kiroku tries to get rid of an erection by banging it on piano keys, or when a kid flings pebbles at an adult's eyes and skates away in a manner that evokes Bugs Bunny cartoons. Such moments contribute to an absurdist tone that tacitly rejects harnessing unruly urges for authoritarian means. But Suzuki also altered the script to make the same point in more sinister ways. He added Kiroku's departure for the front to the film's plot, for example; it doesn't appear in the original script by Kaneto Shindo or in the novel on which it is based. The addition makes explicit what is implicit in the original story: Childish play can lead to darker consequences in an ideological atmosphere that seeks to channel that energy into organized violence.

Tadao Sato found significance in another of Suzuki's additions to *Fighting Elegy*. In a brief scene, Kiroku exchanges glances with an older man in a coffee shop. We learn later that this character is Ikki Kita, a real-life right-wing ideologue who inspired a failed military coup in 1936 and was executed for it in 1937. According to Sato, "Since Suzuki detested the constructive, interest in ideology would not have been his reason for inserting the scene. He probably saw in Kita a pathetic symbol for human beings rushing headlong to their deaths in the coming world war." These final scenes shift the film to a somber, ironic tone, in shocking contrast to the humor that pervades the rest of it, giving us "a fleeting glimpse of the serious side of Seijun Suzuki."[118]

STORY OF A PROSTITUTE

Based on a Taijiro Tamura novel that had been made into a hit film called *Escape at Dawn* in 1950, *Story of a Prostitute* is set in Manchuria during the Sino-Japanese War. Its heroine, Harumi (Yumiko Nogawa), is one of seven comfort women sent to service a garrison of some one thousand Japanese troops. She faces brutality at the hands of a lieutenant who wants to make her his exclusive property and carries on a clandestine affair with his aide Shinkichi (Tamio Kawaji), landing them in trouble that only gets worse when the Chinese army attacks their outpost. It is, in part, a classic *giri/ninjo* story in that Shinkichi is caught between his love for Harumi and his duty to uphold his battalion's honor. The film's main theme, though, is that codes such as these are meant to thwart natural human desire. As Suzuki put it in an interview, "In drama ... you need some kind of moral code or something binding that the characters either submit to or resist. ... As an army has its own code, prostitutes have their own code. Characters bound by such a code either resist it or submit to it."[119] Harumi and Shinkichi resist and suffer for it.

Directed by Senkichi Taniguchi and written by Akira Kurosawa, *Escape at Dawn* was praised as a sensitive antiwar drama, but it sanitized the story by making the women entertainers rather than prostitutes. By restoring the women to their original roles and emphasizing the soldiers' sexual appetites, Suzuki turned the story into one of people crushed by the imposed morals of the military. Working in the B movie medium, which encouraged titillation and gave him latitude to experiment, allowed Suzuki to slip his anti-authori-

By restoring the women to their original roles and emphasizing the soldiers' sexual appetites, Suzuki turned the story into one of people crushed by the imposed morals of the military.

tarian message through more forcefully than Taniguchi could have done. His florid style emphasizes the ludicrousness of war. *Story of a Prostitute*'s lurid atmosphere and excesses of sex and violence led critics at the time to accuse Suzuki of being exploitative, but Sato regarded it as a true image of Japan during the war.[120]

In a typically cryptic statement about this windswept film set in the desert, Suzuki said, "God is wind. It transcends human beings, making them as insignificant as insects."[121] Considering his embrace of nihilism and destruction, I rather doubt that Suzuki has any firmly held religious beliefs.[122] Instead, I think he was connecting the film's message to his nihilist philosophy (recall his quote: "love, living together, getting married and dying is no more than a gust of wind blowing past your head"). Harumi and Shinkichi are insignificant cogs in the military machine, the army itself is subject to the whims of those with power (not to mention its enemies), and all are, in the end, just playthings for God's amusement.[123]

GATE OF FLESH

If we all are playthings for God's amusement (and God is nothing but wind), maybe the road to utopia runs through the "gate of flesh" and transcendence is achieved by indulging in earthly pleasures. If Suzuki never went so far as to articulate this credo, Taijiro Tamura, author of the novels on which

Opposite: Fig. 68 A scene lit with a spotlight in *Gate of Flesh*

Figs. 69, 70 *Gate of Flesh*

both *Story of a Prostitute* and *Gate of Flesh* are based, certainly did. *Gate of Flesh* is the most famous of the novels he published beginning in 1946 "extolling the truth and honesty of *nikutai*, or 'flesh,' as opposed to the delusions of abstract 'thought' or 'ideas.'" From the mid-nineteenth century through the end of World War II, "all Japanese had been indoctrinated to believe that the supreme object of veneration was the *kokutai*, or emperor-centered 'national entity.'" With the war over and the nation defeated, Tamura declared through his writings that "the only body deserving of veneration was the 'flesh' (*niku*)—the sensual body—of the individual. The abstract 'nation body' or nation state was meaningless, and all patriotic blather about it was duplicitous."[124]

Gate of Flesh was made into a hit play in 1947, so it's fitting that Suzuki's film version should be so theatrical, including not only histrionic acting and production design that looks like stage sets but theatrical lighting effects such as spotlights (fig. 68). Jo Shishido's Shintaro embodies Tamura's philosophy with his lust for food, women, and drink. He declares at one point that he doesn't believe in anything he can't put his hands on. In a voiceover, Maya calls Tokyo a "city of savages." The film makes clear that these characters on the bottom rung of postwar society have embraced a philosophy of self-reliance out of necessity: They have nothing but their bodies to rely on.

The blame for this desperate situation is placed on the American occupying forces, who were inextricably linked to the underground economy of black marketeering and prostitution that *Gate*'s characters are caught up in. In keeping with *Gate of Flesh*'s blunt, even crass symbolism, one character finds a condom in something he is eating called "American Stew," and one of the prostitutes' clients is an American priest. In an interview for *Gate of Flesh*'s American DVD release, Suzuki said that being on a ship that sunk during an American air raid made him hate the United States and that the American flag was "a symbol of my grudge."[125] The flag appears twice in the film, once while a character declares that "we should spit on everything," and again in the film's final scene, flying over a slum (fig. 69) just after a shot of a Japanese flag lying in a filthy canal (fig. 70).

Suzuki's remark was delivered with a smile to an American interviewer some five decades after the war's end. It is an example of Suzuki's way of being genial and provocative at once, and an indication that tensions had dissipated enough by that time that they could be spoken about openly. But it is also an honest reflection of how he and other Japanese people felt about Americans during the postwar occupation.

Though Tamura's novel *Gate of Flesh* was a bestseller, Suzuki's film version was, according to critic Max Tessier, "heavily criticized in Japan for its

excesses, its sadomasochism and its lack of 'humanitarianism.'" He links the film's controversial elements to Suzuki's "personal vision":

> What also shocked the Japanese was that twenty years after the defeat, Suzuki refused to appeal to the Japanese "victim-consciousness" and affirmed the "I" and the primacy of the body, of brute animal life force over any form of spirituality or morality.
>
> Sex and the drive to kill are closely linked, as they are in Oshima's or Imamura's films, but all these elements are here fused into a baroque aesthetic with a hyper-spectacular *mise-en-scene*. In a sense, it is the antithesis of Kurosawa's humanism or of the other progressivist film makers of the time: in their films, Man had to be redeemed through hope whereas Suzuki stresses basic instincts, the lack of any ideal, of a moral cause.[126]

After the war, military uniforms and boots became known as "defeat suits" and "defeat shoes," children's songs were refashioned with cynical lyrics about the dangers of postwar Tokyo, and pious wartime phrases such as "thanks to our fighting men" quickly became "a bitter, nasty comment on how Japan had come to find itself in its current predicament."[127] *Gate of Flesh* captures this strain of bitter survival-humor, and *Fighting Elegy* and *Story of a Prostitute* apply it retrospectively to the war and its buildup. Their B movie aesthetics are perhaps better suited to express this cynical mockery of authority than more prestigious films might have been. ●

116 Richie, *A Hundred Years of Japanese Film*, 180.

117 Teo, "Seijun Suzuki: Authority in Minority."

118 Sato, *Currents in Japanese Cinema*, 229.

119 Suzuki, "Interview," *Story of a Prostitute*.

120 Sato, "Interview," *Story of a Prostitute*.

121 Suzuki, "Suzuki on Suzuki," 27.

122 If he does, they are in keeping with his extreme pessimism. He once wrote, "I have a feeling there is a god, but not a visible one, as in Buddhism or Christianity. I'm thinking more of an evil spirit." Suzuki, "Suzuki on Suzuki," 28.

123 Sato attributes this quote to Suzuki. Sato, "Interview," *Story of a Prostitute*.

124 John W. Dower, *Embracing Defeat: Japan in the Wake of World War II* (New York: W. W. Norton & Company, Inc., 1999), 157–58.

125 Suzuki, "Interview," *Gate of Flesh*.

126 Suzuki, Willemen, and Sato, *The Films of Seijun Suzuki*, 38.

127 Dower, *Embracing Defeat*, 171.

7

AMERICAN CONNECTIONS

That we see more passion and political commentary in Suzuki's war films suggests that they are more imbued with personal feeling than many of his others. His experiences surrounding World War II clearly colored the way he approached this material and, in a larger sense, the way he conducted his career and structured his films. I find interesting parallels in this regard between Suzuki and two American artists whose disdain for authority and desire to buck narrative conventions also stem from their wartime experiences.

SUZUKI AND SAMUEL FULLER

Virtually everyone who writes about Suzuki points out that the American director closest to him in sensibility is Samuel Fuller. Born in 1912 in Worcester, Massachusetts, he moved with his family to New York City at a young age. Before becoming a filmmaker, he worked as a reporter for New York's tabloid newspapers, writing lurid stories about crimes in the city's seedy underbelly.

Like Suzuki, Fuller fought in World War II, seeing heavy combat as an infantryman in Europe and Africa, landing on Omaha Beach on D-Day, and participating in the liberation of the concentration camps. Also like Suzuki, he returned home to make B movies with a distinct personal flair, wrangled with studio bosses, and at times found himself out of work because of his stubbornness. Martin Scorsese's admiring description of his films as "blunt, pulpy, occasionally crude"[128] could just as easily apply to Suzuki's.

The war turned Fuller less into a nihilist than a ruthlessly pragmatic, hard-boiled ironist with a keen sense of social justice. But the war instilled in both men a deep cynicism toward authority, great sympathy for the underdog, and a rebellious streak that comes through both in their films and in

Opposite: Samuel Fuller's *Pickup on South Street*. Photofest

their battles with studios. Fuller's attitude comes across in a quote from an interview with Roger Ebert: "Even World War II, with all its idealism ... there was a lot of hypocrisy. Because basically, what the rich were saying was, 'We loaned a lot of money to Europe that we're never going to get back if Hitler wins.' ... But what was sad was that they waved the flag and let the band play for a bunch of young men to go fight a war, and never gave them a piece of the corporation called the country."[129]

Fuller honed the same "genre hack" skills as Suzuki did and at times was able to use them to criticize American postwar ideology, just as Suzuki criticized that of his own country. For me, there are informative similarities between *Gate of Flesh* and Fuller's *Pickup on South Street* (1953). Both express anger at their respective postwar societies through marginal, criminal characters whose amoral behavior is somehow more worthy of admiration than the power structures of the status quo.

Fuller's film stars Richard Widmark as Skip, a pickpocket who happens upon some microfilm that was on its way to a communist spy, leading to entanglements with the police, federal agents, and the communists. Widmark's Skip is just as much the amoral scoundrel as Shishido's Shintaro is in *Gate of Flesh*. Lacking leverage to arrest him but convinced that he has the microfilm, the authorities appeal to Skip's patriotic duty to turn it over, prompting his famous response: "Are you waving the flag at me?" Delivered in a movie made in the thick of Cold War paranoia, this is an altogether remarkable line. Rather than giving in to what he calls "patriotic eyewash," Skip instead tries to play everyone off of each other so he can get the top dollar for his prize. "I got no problem doing business with a Red," he says at one point, displaying a mercenary attitude similar to Shintaro's, who in *Gate of Flesh* has no qualms about selling counterfeit medicine on the black market.

In another film made during that time of anti-communist propaganda, Skip might have been the villain; but in *Pickup on South Street*, a film that depicts America as awash in paranoia, he is, in a weird way, the hero. Everyone in the film is being watched or followed by someone else, and, in Fuller's cynical worldview, everyone—from the cops who pay for information to Skip and his underworld crowd—is running a con. All noble ideals have been compromised by the Red Scare, and anything or anyone can be bought for the right price.

The film is suffused with a disillusionment that is just as profound, if not as desperate, as *Gate of Flesh*'s is. Thelma Ritter gives a priceless performance as Moe, a career stool pigeon who calls herself a "solid citizen"; she just happens to get paid for it. She says of Skip, "He's slippery as smoke, but

I love him." To which another character responds, "You just sold him out for sixty bucks!"

Happy endings for criminal characters were expressly forbidden in studio films at the time in America and Japan. Redemption, punishment, and death were the only options. Despite these restrictions, Fuller managed to finesse the ending of his film quite elegantly. Skip ultimately redeems himself by doing the right thing and turning the microfilm over—not out of patriotism, but out of loyalty to Moe and his other underworld cohorts. In the nihilist end of *Gate of Flesh*, on the other hand, the other prostitutes ostracize Shintaro and Maya for falling in love. As the couple tries to escape, Shintaro is gunned down during a black market double-cross, and Maya is left on her own. The stakes are different in poor postwar Japan and affluent postwar America, but both directors used genre cinema to deliver sustained attacks on the injustices of their respective societies within the political constraints of commercial moviemaking.

SUZUKI AND KURT VONNEGUT

There are also intriguing parallels between Suzuki and the American novelist Kurt Vonnegut. As a prisoner of war during World War II, Vonnegut witnessed the firebombing of Dresden. He later used that experience as the springboard for his most famous novel, *Slaughterhouse-Five* (1969). In its own way, Vonnegut's attitude toward the war was as perverse as Suzuki's. Because of the success of *Slaughterhouse-Five*, he called himself the only person who benefited from the firebombing, in which as many as 25,000 people died: "I got three dollars for every person killed. Imagine that."[130]

Vonnegut began his career in the literary equivalent of the B movie studios: writing short stories for magazines, which, in those days, actually

> He [Vonnegut] seems to have taken a similarly workmanlike approach to these pieces and, like Suzuki, experimented with form while maintaining respect for narrative mechanics and the necessity of pleasing his audience.

paid decent money for them. He seems to have taken a similarly workmanlike approach to these pieces and, like Suzuki, experimented with form while maintaining respect for narrative mechanics and the necessity of pleasing his audience. He once noted, "I guarantee you that no modern story scheme, even plotlessness, will give a reader genuine satisfaction, unless one of those old-fashioned plots is smuggled in."[131] Compare this to Suzuki's comments on the reasoning behind the snow imagery in *Kanto Wanderer*, insisting that it was necessary to the scene as opposed to serving as a symbol in some "absurd experimental film."

It's not just that Vonnegut and Suzuki molded pulp forms into something new; they exploded them in order to expose their workings. We already saw that destruction, for Suzuki, is the ultimate power. So too for Vonnegut, who saw an entire city turned to charred rubble around him. Billy Pilgrim, the hero of *Slaughterhouse-Five*, famously becomes "unstuck in time," enabling Vonnegut to create a fragmented narrative that skips around chronologically while maintaining plot threads that owe much to his early sci-fi pulp-work. Similarly, the narratives of Suzuki's Nikkatsu films became increasingly unstuck from logic, exploding completely with *Branded to Kill*, just as the imagery of snow, wind chimes, and burning leaves is unstuck from the seasons in *Kanto Wanderer*.

These parallels highlight a common sensibility shared by two affable nihilists[132] forged on opposite sides of the same war. After witnessing destruction, they used it as a structuring principle. Destruction is not just the subject of *Slaughterhouse-Five* and *Branded to Kill*: it is the motivation behind them. Simply parodying the absurdity of war through conventional narrative forms, as in Joseph Heller's *Catch-22* or any number of war films, wasn't enough. Suzuki and Vonnegut had to expose the workings of those structures to emphasize their absurdity and show the hidden powers behind them. And let's not forget that *Branded to Kill* and *Slaughterhouse-Five* were the works that made each of their creators heroes to the countercultures of their respective countries—countercultures neither of them could fully embrace, knowing that the utopias they were chasing were destined for destruction as well. ●

After witnessing destruction, they used it as a structuring principle. Destruction is not just the subject of *Slaughterhouse-Five* and *Branded to Kill*: it is the motivation behind them.

128 Samuel Fuller, *A Third Face: My Tale of Writing, Fighting and Filmmaking* (New York: Alfred A. Knopf, 2003), ix.

129 Roger Ebert, "'All War Stories are Told by Survivors': An Interview with Sam Fuller," accessed May 12, 2015, http://www.rogerebert.com/interviews/all-war-stories-are-told-by-survivors-an-interview-with-samuel-fuller

130 David Hayman et al., "Kurt Vonnegut: The Art of Fiction No. 64," *The Paris Review*, accessed April 21, 2015, http://www.theparisreview.org/interviews/3605/the-art-of-fiction-no-64-kurt-vonnegut

131 David Hayman et al., "Kurt Vonnegut: The Art of Fiction No. 64."

132 Vonnegut referred to his lifelong Pall Mall chain-smoking habit as "a classy way to commit suicide."

8

HIATUS AND RETURN

After Suzuki was fired by Nikkatsu in 1968, none of the five major Japanese film studios would hire him. They effectively colluded to ban him from making movies. Even after he won his lawsuit for wrongful dismissal, "the cartel of major production companies continued blacklisting him until 1977."[133] To earn a living, he turned to directing commercials and won an award for one of them in 1969. He wrote a number of books, starting with a volume that included the screenplay for *Fighting Elegy* and a selection of poems in 1970, and made a guest appearance in Kazuki Omori's 1975 film *I Can't Wait Until Dark*. Considering that his firing had the effect of making him more famous than ever, I asked him if he missed feature filmmaking during this time. With typical nonchalance, he responded that there was nothing he could do about it, so he didn't let it bother him.[134]

Based on the self-deprecation, eccentricity, and impish charm he exuded in his writings and speeches from his time away from filmmaking, one can see how he became such a beloved public figure in Japan. "'Here lies the third rate,' is the epitaph my wife has thought up for me," he remarked during his testimony supporting Nagisa Oshima's obscenity trial for *In the Realm of the Senses*, going on to note that even though he was a "third-rate" director, Oshima still treated him with respect.[135] In a 1972 speech introducing a screening of *Kanto Wanderer*, he delivered another self-putdown:

> When I arrived here, looked at the brochure and saw the title of the lecture series, *Ideas on Japanese Cinema*, I was rather surprised. You will understand this now that you see my face, which doesn't exactly radiate ideas. It's my opinion that, from the first, there really haven't been any ideas in Japanese cinema.

He then went on to disparage *Kanto Wanderer* as just a typical yakuza film, listed several other yakuza films he thought were better than his, and

Opposite: *A Tale of Sorrow and Sadness*. See page 106.

concluded by positing that the reason the film was being shown instead of others that night was "undoubtedly the presence of 'ideas' in [*Kanto Wanderer*]! This implies that it doesn't matter if a film is boring, as long as it embodies an idea."[136]

A TALE OF SORROW AND SADNESS

The rather inaptly titled *A Tale of Sorrow and Sadness* (1977) was Suzuki's return to directing after a ten-year hiatus. Written by Atsushi Yamatoya—one of the eight members of *Guryu Hachiro* (Group of Eight), including Suzuki and Kimura, who were credited with the screenplay for *Branded to Kill*—*Tale* is a soft-core porn melodrama. Yoko Shiraki stars as Reiko, a model who is groomed to become a professional golfer as a publicity stunt and subsequently falls victim to a deranged fan's blackmail plot.

A box office flop on release, *Tale* was for many years ignored until a DVD release in the early 2000s, which spurred some critics to re-evaluate it. Jasper

Fig. 71 *A Tale of Sorrow and Sadness*

Sharp, reviewing it for *Midnight Eye*, described the film as "riddled with the director's wildly non-conformist use of non-contiguous edits, unhinged shot composition, and violent splashes of colour. ... this long-overlooked work simply cries out for revival."[137] Touches of Suzuki's stylistic individuality flare up here and there (as does Jo Shishido, in a cameo role), particularly in the eccentric use of color: Reiko's apartment has sickly green walls, and her fingernails go from yellow to black as the film progresses ("because her mood changes," according to Suzuki[138]).

In terms of inventiveness, though, *Tale* represents a step back from *Tokyo Drifter* and *Branded to Kill*. It's more of a return to the style of Suzuki's earlier

Nikkatsu films: enlivening a linear narrative form—a critique of celebrity and the sports industry with a few nude scenes tossed in for titillation—with sparks of invention. Watching it is a bit of an uncanny experience. One has to wonder how much of the flamboyant costume and production design came from Suzuki and how much owes to the late 1970s era that had absorbed flamboyance into mainstream fashion and design. Green bedroom walls would have looked very bizarre indeed in 1965, but by 1977 they wouldn't have been out of place in a modern apartment (fig. 71), along with an avocado refrigerator or a brown stove.

LUPIN III: LEGEND OF THE GOLD OF BABYLON

A more triumphant, if unconventional, return would come three years later with *Zigeunerweisen*, the first film of the Taisho Trilogy. Between making the second and third films in the trilogy, Suzuki was involved in two other productions that, like *A Tale of Sorrow and Sadness*, have come to be regarded as orphans in his filmography and are rarely shown or discussed. *Lupin III: Legend of the Gold of Babylon* (1985) is the only anime feature Suzuki worked on (co-directing with Shigetsugu Yoshida, with whom he also directed a fifty-episode television series, featuring the same main character, in 1984).

Lupin III is supposed to be the grandson of Arsene Lupin, the gentleman thief created by French crime writer Maurice Leblanc. The character made his debut in a manga comic book in the late 1960s, which turned into a franchise encompassing hundreds of television episodes, several anime features, and, recently, a big-budget live action feature. There's no identifiable Suzukian touch in *Lupin III: Legend of the Gold of Babylon*,[139] essentially a work-for-hire gig that may have benefitted from his name recognition.

CAPONE CRIES A LOT

Interestingly, both *Lupin III* and *Capone Cries A Lot*, Suzuki's other orphaned feature of 1985, take place in the United States. Unlike *Babylon*, *Capone* is a live action feature that is very much a Suzuki film, though it is lighter in touch than the Taisho films that bookend it. Based on a 1975 novel by the popular writer Kajiyama Toshiyuki, its script is credited to Atsushi Yamatoya and Takeo Kimura. The rather absurd story involves Kaiemon, a performer of *naniwa-bushi* (a style of traditional singing popular in early twentieth-century Japan) who moves to Prohibition-era San Francisco in the hope of making it as a star in America. Mistakenly believing that Al Capone is the president, Kaiemon's dream is to sing for him and thus popularize his art form.

I suspect that *Capone* is an orphan in Suzuki's oeuvre for more troublesome reasons than is *Tale* or *Lupin III*. To call it a "blackface gangster curio," as Chuck Stephens did,[140] is a disservice at the very least, but there are some borderline racist scenes involving a buffoonish African-American character, and a minstrel band in blackface shows up in a couple of scenes. It may be that Suzuki was less squeamish about showing these things than an American director would have been, as he was removed from the deep-seated sensitivities they can provoke and Japanese audiences were less likely to take offense. Distasteful as they are, minstrel shows were, after all, an actual form of entertainment in the 1920s. To me, though, whatever whiffs of racism cling to those characters are balanced by a real African-American jazz ensemble (anachronistically wearing contemporary hairstyles and clothing) that plays a much larger role in the film than the minstrels do, at several points even performing with Kaiemon in fusions of blues, jazz, and *naniwa-bushi*.

Though set mostly in the United States, *Capone* was filmed entirely in Japan, forcing Suzuki and Kimura to be especially inventive with their art direction and set design.

Though set mostly in the United States, *Capone* was filmed entirely in Japan, forcing Suzuki and Kimura to be especially inventive with their art direction and set design. They used an abandoned amusement park to create a very strange idea of Prohibition-era San Francisco, chockablock with advertising billboards for candy bars and boxing matches, and populated with gangsters and cowboys—cartoonish caricatures who seem to owe their lineage to the way Edo-period Japanese artists caricatured visiting westerners as "southern barbarians."[141] This artificial world allows for all kinds of cultural mash-ups. Kaiemon's friend Gun Tetsu muscles in on the Capone brothers' bootlegging operation with his own sake racket. Kaiemon sings *naniwa-bushi* songs about the sad plight of the Native Americans, impersonates Charlie Chaplin, and in an operatic finale, both sings for and battles Al Capone himself. Despite its more discomfiting elements, *Capone* may be even more worthy of re-evaluation than *A Tale of Sorrow and Sadness*.

Another factor that has made these films anomalies in Suzuki's oeuvre is a lack of proper distribution. *A Tale of Sorrow* disappeared for several years after it flopped at the box office. *Capone* has never been available commercially in the United States. They rarely appear in Suzuki retrospectives. These films are transitional works that complicate the narrative of Suzuki's career, stylistically falling between his studio work at Nikkatsu and the independent Taisho Trilogy films that revived his reputation. ●

133 Tony Rayns, "Biography," in *Branded to Thrill: The Delirious Cinema of Suzuki Seijun* (London: British Film Institute, 1995), 46.

134 Suzuki, email to the author (translated by Yuka Sakano), February 19, 2014.

135 Suzuki, "Cinema, Film Directors and Oshima," 45.

136 Suzuki, "The Days of Kanto Mushuku," 39–40.

137 Jasper Sharp, "A Tale of Sorrow and Sadness," accessed April 21, 2015, http://www.midnighteye.com/reviews/story-of-sorrow-and-sadness/

138 Suzuki and Ueno, "Forgetting Foreign Names," 71.

139 This piece gives some general background on Lupin III, including the author's attempt to reinterpret *Babylon* after he realized who Suzuki was: Michael Toole, "The Mike Toole Show: The Lupin Tapes," accessed April 21, 2015, http://www.anime-newsnetwork.com/the-mike-toole-show/the-lupin-tapes/2010-06-06

140 Chuck Stephens, "Takeo Kimura: 1918–2010," *The Criterion Collection*, accessed April 21, 2015, http://www.criterion.com/current/posts/1433-takeo-kimura-1918-2010

141 Art Institute of Chicago, "Southern Barbarians," accessed April 22, 2015, http://www.artic.edu/aic/collections/citi/resources/Rsrc_001100.pdf

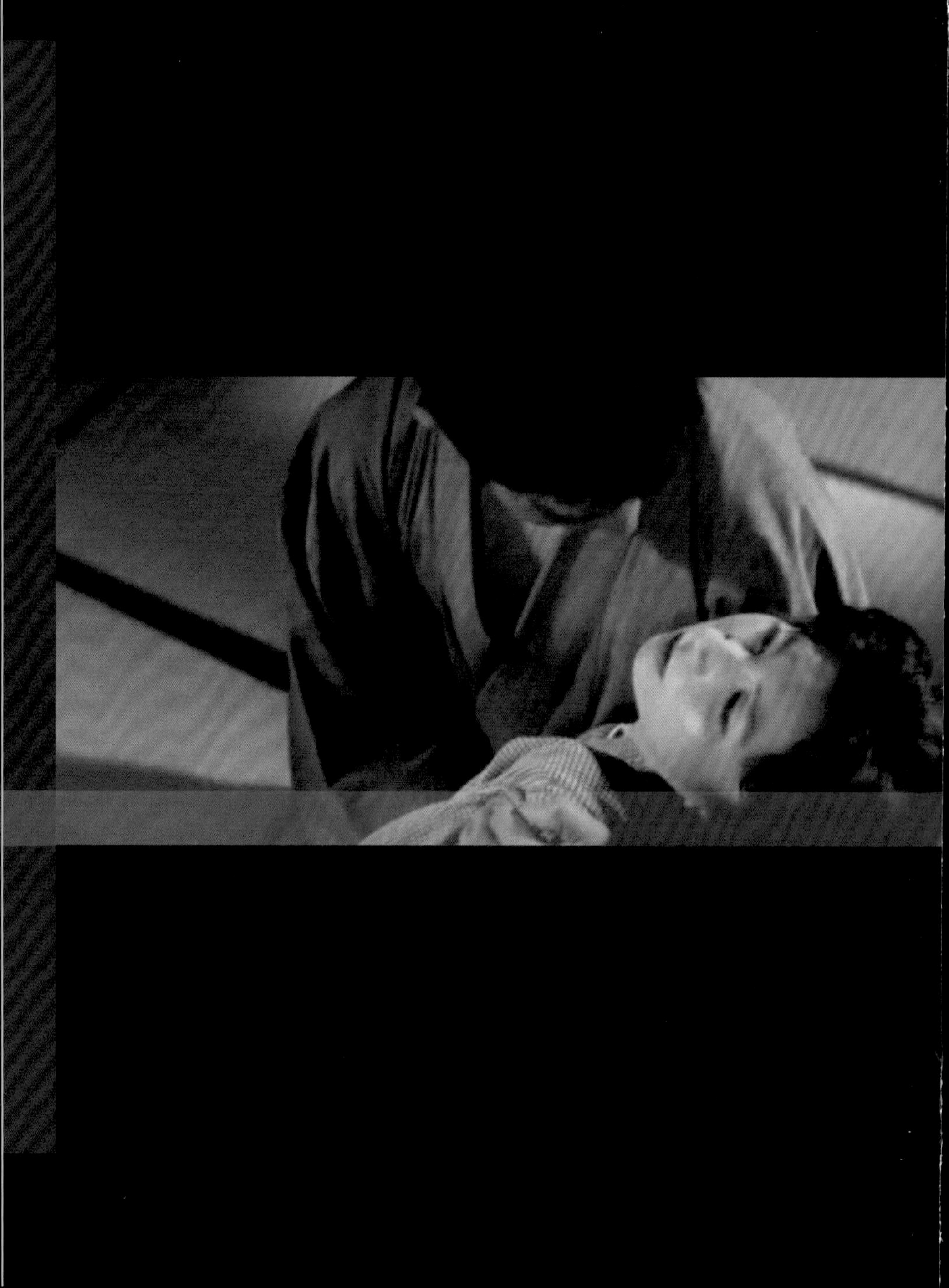

9

TRADITIONAL INFLUENCES

Suzuki's Nikkatsu career has been placed within the artistic, political, and social context of the times. But even what has been identified in his work as avant-garde, modernist, postmodernist, or somewhere in between has deep roots in Japanese aesthetic traditions that Suzuki, a Kabuki and *ukiyo-e* enthusiast and reader of the Japanese classics, often knowingly employed. He especially drew on these traditions in the Taisho Trilogy films, along with *Pistol Opera* and *Princess Raccoon.*

LITERARY ANTECEDENTS

Any number of commentators has placed Suzuki in the context of the *ero guro nansensu* (erotic grotesque nonsense) movement in art and literature, which was devoted to extreme images of violence and sexual decadence. Born in the Taisho period, this tradition is closely identified with the horror writer known as Edogawa Ranpo (1894–1965), a pen name phonetically evoking "Edgar Allan Poe." Many of his most popular tales were written during the Taisho period, but their gothic perversity resonated with several filmmakers pursuing extreme themes and aesthetics in the 1960s. Yasuzo Masumura adapted one of Ranpo's tales in *Blind Beast* (1969), about a blind sculptor who kidnaps and tortures a model. Kinji Fukasaku adapted the detective story *Black Lizard* in 1968, starring the famous drag queen (and lover of Yukio Mishima) Akihiro Miwa. Teruo Ishii, a stylist as flamboyant as Suzuki, adapted several Ranpo tales for *Horrors of Malformed Men* (1969), a film so controversial it is still banned in Japan.

Tony Rayns and Tadao Sato identify parallels in Suzuki's work with an even longer tradition of satire and bawdiness in Japanese literature. Rayns wrote, "Within the Japanese poetic tradition (*waka*) lurks a counter-tradi-

Opposite: *Kanto Wanderer.*
See page 114.

tion of comic verse known as *kyoka* (literally, 'crazed *waka*')." Intended to subvert seriousness and pretension, these poems parody the *waka* tradition through satire. Rayns called Suzuki the "*kyoka* factor in Japanese movies."[142] Citing the rude humor that pervades Suzuki's work, Sato wrote, "He can be called a *gesakusha*, a humorist whose roots date back to the popular comical literature of the Edo period, for example, *Shank's Mare* by Ikku Jippensha (1765–1831)."[143]

Both of these interpretations make sense to a certain degree. *Kyoka* poets use the rules of *waka* for mockery and subversion, just as Suzuki mocked and subverted the genres he worked in at Nikkatsu. The heroes of *Shank's Mare* are two comical scoundrels traveling from Tokyo to Kyoto, a journey full of the kind of dirty jokes and lowbrow gags Suzuki has employed throughout his career. "Erotic grotesque nonsense" might be a perfect descriptor of *Gate of Flesh* and *Branded to Kill*, as it would be for any number of "extreme" Japanese films from the 1960s through today. But these are all interpretations from the outside—attempts to contextualize Suzuki by comparing him to or placing him within these traditions, rather than looking at how he deliberately threads them through his work.

Kyoka poets use the rules of *waka* for mockery and subversion, just as Suzuki mocked and subverted the genres he worked in at Nikkatsu.

SHUNGA

Considering the eroticism that emerges in his late Nikkatsu films and pervades the later films, from *A Tale of Sadness and Sorrow* through *Pistol Opera*, it's surprising that none of the above commentators attempted to place Suzuki in the tradition of erotic *shunga* woodblock prints. *Shunga* (meaning "spring pictures," "spring" being a traditional euphemism for sex) is the sexually explicit subgenre of the *ukiyo-e* ("pictures of the floating world") prints popular during the Edo period (1615–1868).[144] The most famous example is probably Katsushika Hokusai's *The Dream of the Fisherman's Wife*, in which a woman is graphically pleasured by a pair of octopi.

Suzuki referenced *shunga* at least three times in his oeuvre. In the most Godardian scene of his most Godardian film, *Carmen from Kawachi*, the heroine and her boyfriend dress up as a geisha and a ninja to act in a porn film directed by a business tycoon, who bases their positions on a book of *shunga* prints he keeps by the camera. One of the prevailing conventions of *shunga* is couples engaged in contorted, exaggerated sexual positions while partially draped in elaborately patterned textiles—a clear inspiration for a bizarre sex

Fig. 72 *Kagero-za*

scene in *Kagero-za* (fig. 72). And in *Yumeji*, a female character uses *shunga* prints for what Timon Screech and other scholars have posited as one of their intended uses: masturbation material.

BIJINGA

Suzuki is also a fan of the *bijinga* (roughly, "pictures of beautiful women") genre of Japanese art that runs from the Edo period through today. Suzuki was thinking like a *bijinga* artist himself when he talked about his technique of focusing on the most attractive aspect of an actress[145] or his decision to cast three generations of actresses in *Pistol Opera* to "show the audience how the beauty of women changes over the years."[146]

Bijinga pictures evolved over the centuries, reflecting each era's standards of beauty and particular notions of ideal womanhood. I like to think of films such as *Underworld Beauty* and *Story of a Prostitute* as *bijinga* in motion: portraits of women with the added element of time, inflected with the energy of the era and the unique sensuality and vitality of the actresses. On a strictly

Fig. 73 The sight of a woman's neck...

Fig. 74 ...incites the hero's lust in *Kanto Wanderer*

visual level, there's little relation to the *bijinga* tradition in Suzuki's Nikkatsu phase (for one thing, I can't imagine Mari Shiraki sitting still long enough to strike a traditional pose). But there is a moment in *Kanto Wanderer* when the hero is inflamed with lust at the sight of the nape of a woman's neck peeking out from her kimono—a traditionally erotic image in Japanese art (fig. 73, fig. 74). This moment is a key to his character: his insistence on following the old ways keeps him out of step with modern times.

The nude scenes in *Gate of Flesh* and *Branded to Kill* are so frenetic as to be nearly devoid of eroticism, but they were filmed with careful attention to sensuous lighting and visual beauty. Borrowing a move from his Nikkatsu days, when he would stage his action scenes as extra-diegetic spectacles in themselves, in *A Tale of Sorrow and Sadness* he fulfilled his quota of nude scenes by filming star Yuko Shiraki in poses that have nothing to do with the narrative, as if drawing attention to their gratuitous nature (fig. 75).

Fig. 75 *A Tale of Sorrow and Sadness*

KABUKI

When I asked Suzuki in an email about artists who influenced his visual style, he mentioned Kokei Kobayashi (1883–1957), who painted in a refined, neoclassical style and produced many exquisite *bijinga* images, and Kinzo Hirose (aka Ekin, 1812–1876), who is famous for his colorful, fabulously grotesque paintings of Kabuki scenes.[147] The former choice might seem surprising (though it makes sense in terms of Suzuki's later films). The latter makes perfect sense, not only because Suzuki and Hirose share a taste for the lurid in both subject matter and color, but also because Kabuki is the one element of traditional Japanese culture that Suzuki consistently cites as an influence. He told Katherine Monk, for instance, that his films were modeled on Kabuki: "There are three points: the love scene, the murder scene and the battle scene. Translated into film, those are the three basic ingredients of entertainment."[148] He frequently used the widescreen Cinemascope format in his Nikkatsu films because its dimensions resembled, for him, the dimensions of the Kabuki stage.

Today, Kabuki is an eminently respectable art form, presented in elegant theaters and showcased around the world as one of Japan's grand cultural traditions, but this was not the case for most of its history. The earliest documented mention of Kabuki dates to 1603, when Izumo-No-Okuni, a *miko*, or Shinto shrine priestess, developed a form of dance that she performed in dry riverbeds around Kyoto. Her outrageous mixture of sacred ritual and profane popular dance, featuring bawdy jokes and ghost stories, grew very popular and was adopted by prostitutes as a way to attract clients. It was an art form by and for the common people. The ruling shogunate eventually began to see it as a threat to public morality and issued a series of decrees limiting it. The final one, which banned prostitutes from performing, came in 1629 after two scandals, one involving *daimyo* (feudal lords) hosting entire troupes of Kabuki dancers in their castles, the other a deadly riot during a performance in Kyoto in which two rival samurai factions battled on stage. The removal of courtesans from the stage established the tradition, which still holds today, of having only men perform, with some, known as *onnagata*, specializing in female roles.[149]

Today, Kabuki is an eminently respectable art form, presented in elegant theaters and showcased around the world as one of Japan's grand cultural traditions, but this was not the case for most of its history.

The acting in Kabuki is very ritualized and almost dance-like in its movements. Actors strike poses, called *mie*, which have been likened to close-ups in film in that they focus the attention on one performer for a period of time. In his book on Kabuki, Earle Ernst characterized it as "presentational," as opposed to "representational" theater: "In the presentational theatre, the actor does not lose his identity as an actor. The audience does not regard him as a 'real' person but as an actor acting." In representational theater, on the other hand, "every effort is made to convince the audience that the stage is not a stage and that the actor is not an actor."[150 151] Compare this to the way Nikkatsu filmmakers employed actors such as Akira Kobayashi, Tatsuya Watari, and Jo Shishido for performances in which they are meant to be recognized as themselves, not to bury their personalities in their roles.

Kabuki sets and costumes contribute to this presentational aspect. Elaborate and colorful, they are meant to be admired in their own right, but not necessarily to realistically depict what they are representing. The spectacular scene changes, which can include revolving platforms and elaborate machinery, are to be noticed and marveled at, rather than merely creating the illusion of a new setting.

Kabuki's presentational form also inspires and encourages audience participation, unlike Western theater, in which audiences are expected to quietly observe the performance. As Noel Burch noted, "The Kabuki audience of the eighteenth and nineteenth centuries generally expressed their appreciation by calling out to the actors at the moment of their entrance along the *hanamichi* (a ramp running through the auditorium to the stage). ... This tradition is preserved today by small groups of connoisseurs who occupy the front seats at every performance."[152] Takenobu Watanabe told me that the all-night marathons of Suzuki films he attended in Tokyo in the 1970s reminded him of Kabuki performances. The audiences knew the films so well that they yelled at the screen in anticipation of favorite scenes.[153]

Subject matter in Kabuki plays ranges from the ancient to the contemporary. Inconsistencies and anachronisms are freely accepted by the audience (much as they are by Suzuki's fans). As with Suzuki's films, "much of the Kabuki repertoire is preoccupied with violence and cruelty, but in a lurid, fairground way. ... Like *gesakusha* fiction, which was often erotic, as well as funny and cruel, Kabuki was a grotesque mirror held up against a rigid, oppressive, hierarchical society." Edward Seidensticker related that "the best-loved crimes of the Meiji [a historical period spanning 1868–1912] became material for the theater. ... A murdered woman ... made good theater and good popular fiction, and a murderess was even better."[154]

Kabuki is a bit like Western opera in that you generally go in knowing how the story will turn out. The point is to see how the production treats it, how well the actors perform the proscribed roles, and how they will pull off certain famous scenes and effects. I would venture to say that Nikkatsu Action directors were doing something similar. They weren't in competition to come up with original stories; they were competing to stand out in how they handled the same kind of material over and over again. As Suzuki remarked, "The stories were always the same at Nikkatsu, so two different directors could easily find themselves making the same film. I wanted to make something different. This is something that came naturally out of my work. I didn't intellectualize it."[155]

KABUKI STYLE IN SUZUKI'S FILMS

While researching Kabuki for this book, I came across a description of a famous play called *The Treasury of Loyal Retainers* (*Kanadehon Chushingura*). In one scene, a character named Okaru uses a mirror to look surreptitiously at a letter that another character is reading on the other side of the stage. This example of Kabuki's elaborate staging somehow put me in mind of Suzuki, who often tosses in such improbable devices, so I made a note of it. Sure enough, in *Kanto Wanderer*, a character mentions Okaru's mirror because someone is using a similar trick to cheat at cards in a gambling den.

To my mind, *Kanto* is Suzuki's most Kabuki-like Nikkatsu film, and not just because it name-checks Okaru's mirror. It came to me after attending a performance of the nineteenth-century Kabuki play *Tokaido Yotsuya Kaidan* (often translated as *Ghost Story of Yotsuya*).[156] There is little depth to the staging in Kabuki, and the lighting tends to be very flat and even. Characters not involved in the action generally sit on the stage, just watching the action rather than engaging in the stage business that Western plays employ for realism. I already mentioned that the widescreen format reminded Suzuki of the Kabuki stage. The staging of certain scenes in *Kanto*, particularly those set in Japanese-style interiors, mimic Kabuki in the way he distributed his actors in a basically flat plane and shot them from a low angle, using straight-on horizontal tracking shots to frame them in front of shoji screens or windows (fig. 76).

Fig. 76 *Kanto Wanderer*

There are also ties between *Kanto*'s yakuza storyline and Kabuki: "The Kabuki stage was a space to enact the often violent fantasies of an oppressed

Fig. 77 *The Ballad of Narayama*

people. The same can be said of the yakuza film. Suzuki calls his heroes and heroines 'fictional drop-outs from the rigid conventions of our society.' "[157] Akira Kobayashi's performance as the hero Mitsuo is almost Kabuki-like in its rigidity, and he is meant to seem a bit stiff and old-fashioned: He's one of the few characters who wear traditional Japanese dress, and he stubbornly clings to such notions as duty and honor. Suzuki described the final fight scene of *Kanto* as having a "Kabuki groove." Shigehiko Hasumi emphasized this in his description of the scene: "When the two yakuza, in mortal danger, fall backwards like Kabuki actors and knock down the shoji [screens], the whole screen is suddenly filled with scarlet light, which is cut off almost immediately by a black background and a terrifically intense snowfall."(See figs. 23, 24, 25.)

Director Keisuke Kinoshita had experimented with Kabuki-like effects several years earlier in *The Ballad of Narayama* (1958), but for Hasumi, "Suzuki gives these visual tricks an extraordinary pregnancy, because, aware as he is of the possibilities of the medium, he aims to create as much suspense and action as possible."[158] This is the key difference between Kinoshita and Suzuki. Kinoshita's attempt to mix Kabuki and cinema involved complex, beautifully designed, brightly colored sets that don't hide their artificiality. Though the camera is able to move through them in a cinematic way, the film still comes across at times like a play that is being filmed (fig. 77). Suzuki's achievement with *Kanto* was inserting Kabuki artifice into scenes that remain essentially cinematic in their effect. The "Kabuki groove" supports his ultimate aim of achieving maximum action and suspense, creating a tension between theatrical and cinematic effects that Kinoshita was unable to sustain over the course of an entire feature-length film.

Fight scenes in Kabuki are more like dances, formed of static, ritualized movements. The swords don't clash, and the actors don't even touch each other. It's a series of movements symbolizing combat instead of representing it. Weapons definitely meet flesh in Suzuki's fight scenes, but the movements tend to be highly ritualized, even by the fight choreography standards of the day. The finales of *Tattooed Life* and *Kanto Wanderer* are prime examples, but even in the modern-day set *Teenage Yakuza* (1962), a fight between teenagers is blocked out in a way that draws attention to itself as goofily Kabuki-esque (fig. 78).

More than one person[159] has told me that the standard take on Suzuki back in the day was that he was a run-of-the-mill B movie director who might put one crazy scene in each movie. The more of his movies I see, the less I agree with that characterization. Nevertheless, certain scenes in certain

Fig. 78 *Teenage Yakuza*

Fig. 79 *Story of a Prostitute*

films do draw attention to themselves, such as the one in *Take Aim at the Police Van* with a POV shot through a riflescope, or the moment when the heroine of *Story of a Prostitute* looks at her abuser and visualizes him tearing into pieces (fig. 79). This idea of scenes calling attention to themselves as standalone spectacles relates to Kabuki as well. In the production I saw, the final act opened with an extended dance of fireflies, a dream sequence that barely merits a mention in the lengthy program notes. We were taken out of the action of the play and moved into a separate, irrational place. An earlier scene of characters groping in the "dark" (even though the stage was brightly lit) ended with a tremendous flash of light, as if to say, "Ta-da!" Of course, the actors weren't in the dark at all. The point was to show off their prowess at pantomiming it.

As Japan's dominant theatrical tradition, Kabuki conventions informed early silent Japanese cinema (in the same way Western theatrical conventions dominated early American and European films). When its influence re-emerged in the 1960s, it was as part of a movement to revive the irrational,

Fig. 80 A stagehand in Masahiro Shinoda's *Double Suicide*

unruly elements of Japanese culture as a political and artistic stance. Suzuki was one of a number of directors drawing on Kabuki and other forms of theater at the time. Masahiro Shinoda studied theater at Waseda University before becoming a filmmaker and, like Suzuki, sought to use theatrical effects in cinema. He tapped into the irreverent aspects of the Kabuki tradition in *The Scandalous Adventures of Buraikan* (1970), emphasizing the uncanny, demonic elements of Edo period culture and the essential earthiness and bawdiness of an art form that had become perhaps too rarified. That the film tells the story of disreputable people unsuccessfully rebelling against authority seems deliberately in keeping with the prevailing attitude of the time, after the many failed rebellions of the 1960s.

Shinoda also took an avant-garde approach to classical theater in his 1969 *Double Suicide*. Based on a Bunraku puppet play, it features the traditional black-clad stagehands participating in the film as they would have in the play, and in so doing turns an age-old theatrical convention into an avant-garde gesture (fig. 80). Shinoda, who often spoke with Suzuki about how to translate theatrical effects onto film,[160] was similarly "trying to change not only the content and themes but the basic language of cinema ... He realized the potential to subvert aesthetics, film construction and conventional audience expectations in not just 'art' cinema but through popular entertainment, too."[161]

Where Shinoda resurrects Kabuki in order to make political points in *Buraikan*, its influence shows up in Suzuki's films on a more structural level, as an influence on his staging, design, and action scenes. Kabuki seems to have become part of Suzuki's style because of his longtime interest in it and the opportunities he saw for employing its effects in cinema.

"As for why I used a Kabuki style," Suzuki explained in an interview, "in foreign films the camera stays on the principal character. ... Wherever he goes, the camera is waiting. But we do it differently here [in Japan]. In Kabuki they show everything at once. The interest is in seeing where and how the actors enter and exit. On the other hand, in American films the continuity comes from the movements of the individual characters. That's the big difference. What we make here is a series of pictures, so the movements of any one character [are] secondary."[162] This idea of movies being primarily a "series of pictures" is in keeping with Suzuki's emphasis on the screen as surface, with the characters' movements contributing to the overall visual design. The climactic fight scenes in *Kanto Wanderer* and *Tokyo Drifter*, for example, were filmed using mostly wide shots, de-emphasizing individual characters. The

Fig. 81 A musical number in *Tokyo Drifter*. His shadow can just be made out on the backdrop (left of figure).

heroes (who, in Suzuki's mind, would be the focal point in American films) are subsumed into the action choreography and set design.

In his Nikkatsu films, Suzuki's arsenal of effects used the "wrong" way exposes the machinery of cinema in the same way Kabuki exposes its own stage machinery. Examples include the extreme artifice of the musical numbers in *Tokyo Drifter* (fig. 81), the soliloquies in *Gate of Flesh*, and the rear-projection ocean waves in *The Call of Blood*.

Fig. 82 Frontal staging in *Kagero-za*

Kabuki's presentational aesthetic is even more evident in the Taisho Trilogy, *Pistol Opera*, and *Princess Raccoon*. In both *Kagero-za* and *Yumeji*, there are scenes in which characters, though speaking to each other, face the camera, looking at once into the distance and into themselves—a nod to Kabuki's frontal staging (fig. 82). *Zigeunerweisen* and *Kagero-za* feature scene changes without cuts. A character leaves the scene and another steps in; based on context and dialogue, we understand that we've moved into the past or the future while remaining in the same space. Many scenes in *Pistol Opera*, particularly the battle with Painless Surgeon, seem designed to evoke Kabuki-like spectacle. The declamatory, theatrical acting in all of these films also recalls Kabuki. In the Taisho films, however, Suzuki also intended to conjure up his idea of the aura of the era. ●

142 Rayns, "The Kyoka Factor," 9.

143 Sato, *Currents in Japanese Cinema*, 221.

144 For a full history and analysis of *shunga*, see Timon Screech, *Sex and the Floating World: Erotic Images in Japan 1700–1820* (London: Reaktion Books, 2009).

145 Suzuki, "Interview," *Story of a Prostitute.*

146 Mes, "Japan Cult Cinema Interview: Seijun Suzuki."

147 Suzuki, email to the author (translated by Yuka Sakano), February 19, 2014.

148 Katherine Monk, "Japanese legend sees himself as simple chronicler," accessed April 21, 2015, http://sweetbottom.tripod.com/Articles/Oct161991.html

149 I drew heavily on Benito Ortolani's *The Japanese Theatre* (Princeton: Princeton University Press, 1995) for this potted history.

150 Noel Burch, *To the Distant Observer: Form and Meaning in the Japanese Cinema* (Berkeley: University of California Press, 1979), 70.

151 According to many, including my guide to a Kabuki performance in Tokyo, this is the main reason why women have never successfully retaken the Kabuki stage (though some have tried). The *onnagata* aren't female impersonators per se. They perform as ritualized abstractions of femininity. Apparently, it just doesn't look right when an actual woman tries to pull this off.

152 Burch, *To the Distant Observer*, 70.

153 Watanabe, interview.

154 Edward Seidensticker, *Low City, High City* (New York: Alfred A. Knopf, 1983), 160–61.

155 Ian Buruma, "The Eccentric Imagination of a Genre Filmmaker," in *Branded to Thrill: The Delirious Cinema of Suzuki Seijun* (London: British Film Institute, 1995), 20.

156 Nobuo Nakagawa made it into a movie for Shintoho Studios in 1959.

157 Buruma, "The Eccentric Imagination," 20.

158 Hasumi, "A World without Seasons," 13.

159 The list includes Sato and Ueno, who mentioned it in my interviews with them.

160 Suzuki and Ueno, "Forgetting Foreign Names," 71.

161 Desjardins, *Outlaw Masters of Japanese Film*, 113.

162 By generalizing this statement to include all of Japanese cinema, he also brings to mind Ozu, whose staging methods emphasized characters' entrances and exits before a static camera that never followed them in or out. Schilling, *The Yakuza Movie Book*, 101.

10

THE TAISHO ERA

FOLLOWING THE failure of *A Tale of Sorrow and Sadness*, Suzuki began a more artistically and commercially successful phase of his career with *Zigeunerweisen*. When producer Genjiro Arato was unable to convince exhibitors to show it, he and Suzuki did so themselves, using a portable, inflatable tent. This led *Zigeunerweisen* to a successful commercial run, four Japan Academy Awards, and the title of the best Japanese film of the 1980s in a critics' poll.

Despite the plaudits, *Zigeunerweisen* and the two subsequent films that are together known as the Taisho Trilogy remain the least understood of Suzuki's work outside of Japan. David Chute, without having seen them himself, quoted another critic damning them as "bad fake Fellini"[163]—which is ironic considering that Suzuki once wrote an essay titled "Random Notes on Fellini (or: I don't like it)." Ian Buruma also dismissed the trilogy, claiming that freedom from the constraints of genre work made Suzuki unfocused and self-indulgent.[164] And both of these comments come from a publication celebrating a major retrospective of his films!

The confusion owes to the films' uneasy mix of art house and B movie elements, and their settings during the Taisho era (1912–26), a brief period of Japanese history unfamiliar to many Westerners. They also convey Suzuki's own idiosyncratic ideas about that period, which can make them even more mystifying.

Crowned in 1912 at the age of thirty-two, Emperor Taisho (meaning "Great Righteousness") reigned until his death in 1926. He was afflicted with meningitis as a child and remained sickly for most of his life. The emperor "did not fare well in his studies and was ultimately physically and mentally unfit for most of his reign. ... his poor health and weakness of character—and later his womanizing, drinking, and eccentric behavior—made him a parody of the ideal that the emperor was a 'manifest deity.'"[165 166] With a

Opposite: Detail, *Tipsy, from the series Styles of Contemporary Makeup*. See page 127.

weak emperor at the helm, Japan moved toward democracy. A widening gap between rich and poor allowed socialism, Marxism, and anarchism to gain footholds, and social criticism made its way into popular culture.

With its rapid modernization and its cultural climate of consumerism, decadence, and sexual license, the Greater Taisho era (1910–30) has been compared to America's Jazz Age and Europe's Belle Époque. The *ero guro nansensu* (erotic grotesque nonsense) artistic movement that sprouted in the 1920s crystalized the hedonistic and nihilistic currents running through the culture. These currents perhaps stemmed from the Great Kanto Earthquake, which struck four months after Suzuki was born in 1923, laying waste to Tokyo and killing upward of 100,000 people. While conservatives saw the disaster as divine punishment for Japan's drift toward decadence, others saw a chance for a new beginning. The novelist Junichiro Tanizaki famously said, "Almost simultaneously I felt a surge of happiness which I could not keep down. 'Tokyo will be better for this!' I said to myself."[167] In his very short

The cultural archetypes of the time—the *mobo* (modern boy) and especially his counterpart, the *moga* (modern girl)—were products of the tremendous industrialization, modernization, and influx of Western culture and fashion that began in the Meiji era and embodied the new era of sexual freedom.

story "Death Mask" (1932), about a woman who, even as she elegantly dies in her lover's arms, inspires jealousy among her former paramours, Yasunari Kawabata captures something of the exhausted decadence and sex-and-death obsessions of the time, which also permeate Suzuki's trilogy.

The cultural archetypes of the time—the *mobo* (modern boy) and especially his counterpart, the *moga* (modern girl)—were products of the tremendous industrialization, modernization, and influx of Western culture and fashion that began in the Meiji era and embodied the new era of sexual freedom. *Moga* showed off their figures with Western clothing rather than hiding them in traditional kimonos, and many worked in the new European-style cafes that replaced the teahouses of the Edo period. Unlike the subservient geisha who were basically indentured servants in those teahouses, the cafe girls were an independent workforce, free to grant or withhold sexual favors from their male customers according to their own desires. The iconic literary version of the *moga* was created by Junichiro Tanizaki in his 1924 novel *A Fool's Love* (published in English as *Naomi*). Taken as a child bride by Joji, the book's narrator, and groomed in the latest Western fashions, Naomi eventually slips from his control and transforms herself into an independent, modern woman, inspiring the phenomenon of *Naomishugi* (Naomi-ism)—real-life women who emulated the character's path to independence.

Joji's desire to mold Naomi by pushing her to adopt elements of the new Western trends—he buys her ballroom dancing lessons, for example, and tries to fashion her in the image of silent film star Mary Pickford—exemplifies what Miriam Silverberg called the "principle of montage" that was central to Taisho culture. She defined the principle as an "active and often sophisticated process of moving between pieces chosen from various cultures within and outside Japan."[168] But it was by no means an easy mix. Kendall H. Brown put it well:

> With the growth of an urban, industrial, and increasingly international society, where values were instantly and endlessly discussed in the mass media, Japanese ruminated on the nature of national, social, and cultural identity. An essential question resided in all spheres: how could one be both Japanese and modern, if modernity is defined as Western? Were modernity and Japaneseness antithetical? Or could individuals and society synthesize some new middle ground? If so, how? Might modernity have parallels in Japanese tradition, or, more precisely, in those practices actively being constructed as "tradition"? Stated conversely, did the Japanese past contain the seeds—the antecedents—of modernity?[169]

Fig. 83 *Tipsy, from the series Styles of Contemporary Makeup*; Kobayakawa Kiyoshi (1897–1948); Japan, Showa era, 1930; Woodblock print, ink and color on paper; Robert O. Muller Collection, S2003.8.1092. Courtesy of Freer Gallery of Art and Arthur M. Sackler Gallery, Smithsonian Institution.

The influx of modernity and Western aesthetics also transformed traditional art forms in the Taisho era. During this time, "the traditional category of *bijinga*, paintings of beautiful women, was re-interpreted and presented with the techniques of Western realism, but with an honesty, psychological realism and eroticism unseen before."[170] The disheveled young woman with the come-hither look in Kiyoshi Kobayakawa's 1930 woodblock print *Tipsy* (fig. 83) is almost as iconic an image of Taisho hedonism as is Tanizaki's Naomi. Goyo Hashiguchi combined Western techniques with *ukiyo-e* design principles to create distinctly modern *bijinga*, such as 1920's *Woman in Summer*

Fig. 84 *Woman in Summer Dress*; Hashiguchi Goyo (1880–1921); Japan, Taisho era, 1920; Woodblock print, ink and color on paper; Gift of H. Ed Robison in memory of Ulrike Pietzner-Robison; s1993.49. Courtesy of Freer Gallery of Art and Arthur M. Sackler Gallery, Smithsonian Institution.

Left: Fig. 85 *Courtesan*; Ito Shinsui (1898–1972); Japan, Taisho era, 1916; Woodblock print, ink and color on paper; Robert O. Muller Collection; S2003.8.251. Courtesy of Freer Gallery of Art and Arthur M. Sackler Gallery, Smithsonian Institution.

Above: Fig. 86 *Shamisen-bori*; Takehisa Yumeji (1884–1934); Japan, Showa era, 1938; Woodblock print, ink and color on paper; Robert O. Muller Collection; S2003.8.3677. Courtesy of Freer Gallery of Art and Arthur M. Sackler Gallery, Smithsonian Institution.

Dress (fig. 84), whose subject gazes not at the mirror beside her, but directly at the viewer with disarming self-possession and enigmatic eroticism. The weary way in which the subject of Shinsui Ito's *Courtesan* (1916) (fig. 85) adjusts her hair boldly refers to the toll her profession is taking on her, in contrast to the more idealized portraits of courtesans from earlier eras. Takehisa Yumeji, the subject of the third Taisho film, painted women in traditional kimono, but used Western-influenced techniques that embody the crosscurrents of the era (fig. 86).

Fig. 87 *Yumeji*

Fig. 88 *Kagero-za*

Lush, through-and-through eroticism borrowed from Taisho-era aesthetics suffuses the Taisho Trilogy films. Whether in kimono or Western dress, the women in these films are as mysterious, capricious, and seductive as the ones in Tanizaki and Kawabata's writings, or in Hashiguchi and Kobayakawa's prints. They are ardently desired by the male characters and are often involved in complicated affairs and love triangles. In the Taisho films, shots linger on women in ways that bring to mind Taisho era *bijinga* imagery: women dressing or undressing (fig. 87), washing their hair (fig. 88), or wearing kimono and in traditional poses (fig. 89). The women in the Taisho-era prints by artists such as Hashiguchi and Ito have a self-possessed, preoccupied air about them, as if perhaps they are thinking of the lover they just left or are about to meet. Like Hashiguchi and Ito's subjects, the women in Suzuki's Taisho films carry themselves with an erotic mysteriousness that fits with the dreamlike atmosphere. Shigehiko Hasumi elaborated on Suzuki's interest in the Taisho:

Fig. 89 *Zigeurnerweisen*

> It is remarkable that Suzuki has a preference for a time when idealistic anarchism, activistic romanticism and cosmopolitanism were blended into an ambiguous whole; a time when young people, caught between religion and love, experienced the fantasy of freedom for the first time ...
>
> When Suzuki tries to revive the atmosphere of his youth, he does not wallow in melancholy nostalgia. More than anything, he wants to do justice to the coincidence of his being born during that era. Perhaps this was the fate of his generation, that enjoyed intellectual freedom while at the same time being caught between the Meiji and Showa era ...
>
> The radical way in which he rejects all political stances, the ever present dynamics of his leaning toward self-destructiveness and the modesty with which his pervasive lyricism banishes all sentimentality, are all simply steps he takes to make the best of his being born during the Taisho period.[171]

The Taisho era is of interest to Suzuki almost as a poetic concept rather than an historical period. In the Taisho films, there are anarchists and rumors of anarchists. There is a mix of Japanese and European costumes and sets. But these elements are just the basis from which Suzuki launched his stories into imaginative realms beyond the facts of the time. His perspective on the Taisho era came from growing up in the increasingly militarized Showa era—which brought an abrupt end to the Taisho's decadence and energy—and seeing a revival of Taisho style rebellion and radical politics in the 1960s. He told Mark Schilling, "The Taisho was a period that glorified freedom ... within certain boundaries the common people were free. There were anarchists, Bolshevists, terrorists."[172]

For the first two Taisho films, Suzuki adapted the work of writers who extended the destabilized nature of life in the Taisho era into realms of the supernatural. Hyakken Uchida, whose work inspired *Zigeunerweisen*, managed to write stories that feel like descriptions of dreams without becoming as boring as those tend to be in real life. Izumi Kyoka, on whose work Suzuki based *Kagero-za*, specialized in uncanny gothic tales poised between the worlds of the living and the dead. Tony Rayns claimed that what distinguishes Suzuki's Taisho films from the European "art films" of Bergman, Resnais, Antonioni, and the like is that Suzuki's "spread themselves out under the sign of the irrational. It's impossible to 'decode' their mysteries, because the mystery itself is the core of their appeal."[173] The same description could apply to the work of Uchida and Kyoka.

As a temperamental nihilist, Suzuki saw the Taisho period as dominated by "transience, nihilism and decay," whose "colors dominated the Taisho era." The period is a touchstone for the nihilism and anarchy that propel his own work, and he is well-versed in its expressions in Taisho art and politics:

> Nihilism was expressed very strongly in *Daibosatsu toge* (*The Mountain Pass*), a novel by Nakazato Kaisan from the start of the Taisho era. The saying: "If you want to sing, then sing; if you want to die, then die," is about as clear as you can get. ... I don't know where the outer limits of nihilism are, but it seems to me that ... it took the form of self-destruction during the Taisho era. A frequent response to nihilism is anarchy, and you could say that the Taisho era wrote the book for anarchy. One of my favourite sayings is: "I admire the spirit, but I abhor all theories about it," by [Taisho period anarchist] Osuge Sakae. I feel exactly the same way. After all, only that which comes straight from the spirit is real. If you classify it with a certain system or theory, it invariably becomes false, unreal.
>
> Thus, terrorist actions are nothing more than the result of impulses from the human spirit, and not from some theory or system. It's the same with film. A film is the result of an explosion of feelings and emotions, and it's completely unnecessary to supply it with arguments.[174]

This conflation of filmmaking and terrorism is Suzuki at his most provocative. His interviews and writings around the time he was making the Taisho films suggest that coming into his own as a revered independent filmmaker emboldened him to make such kinds of pronouncements. At any rate, the idea of a film as an "explosion of feelings and emotions" is an apt approach to the Taisho films, which exist under the sign of the irrational and resist interpretation at every turn. ●

163 Chute, "Branded to Thrill," 17.

164 Buruma, "The Eccentric Imagination," 23.

165 Sharon A. Minichiello, "Greater Taisho: Japan 1900–1930," in *Taisho Chic* (Honolulu: Honolulu Academy of Arts, 1995), 9.

166 Suzuki liked to joke that Taisho was the most impressive Japanese emperor because he was too weak and feeble-minded to start any wars, unlike the more illustrious emperors Meiji and Showa, whose reigns bracketed Taisho's. Ueno, interview.

167 Michael Hoffman, "The Taisho Era: When Modernity Ruled Japan's Masses," *The Japan Times,* accessed April 21, 2015, http://www.japantimes.co.jp/life/2012/07/29/general/the-taisho-era-when-modernity-ruled-japans-masses/#.U0o_U-b3dbw

168 Miriam Silverberg, *Erotic Grotesque Nonsense: The Mass Culture of Japanese Modern Times* (Berkeley: University of California Press, 2009), 4.

169 Kendall H. Brown, "Flowers of Taisho: Images of Women in Japanese Society and Art, 1915–1935," in *Taisho Chic,* (Seattle: University of Washington Press, 2002), 17.

170 Jackie Menzies, "Exoticism," in *Modern Boy Modern Girl* (New South Wales: Art Gallery of New South Wales, 1998), 132.

171 Hasumi, "A World without Seasons," 24.

172 Schilling, *The Yakuza Movie Book,* 103.

173 Rayns, "The Kyoka Factor," 8.

174 Seijun Suzuki, "The Desert under the Cherry Tree," 60.

11

SUZUKI'S TAISHO TRILOGY

I FIND THE irrationality of the Taisho Trilogy films refreshing in this age of online plot synopses and television recaps. Silicon Valley problem-solving methods seem to have influenced the way we consume films and television, as if even a deliberately open-ended work can be solved like a puzzle if we just acquire enough data. Suzuki's Taisho films are a healthy reminder that art is more than the sum of the information it contains. In all three, plots begin on already shaky ground and dissolve into mystery. Their power is in their uncanny brew of mysteriousness and absurdity. All were produced independently and made outside the confines of the studio, so they give free rein to Suzuki's impulses and have the palpability of being filmed out in the world. Somehow, by being placed in the real world, these ghost stories become even more ghostly.

Though not linked by plot, the films in the Taisho Trilogy all center on what Rayns termed "love/sex/death enigmas."[175] There are torrid affairs and suicide pacts, doppelgangers and ghosts, roving eccentrics and tormented artists. The cultural trends of the time—the mix of Eastern and Western art and fashion, the fascination with the supernatural, the political extremes and obsession with romantic decadence—are further elaborated into a hallucinatory world in which living and dead, past and present, and waking life and dreaming bleed into one another. The deliberate artifice of the acting recalls Kabuki, and the titillation of Suzuki's Nikkatsu films is replaced with the earthy sexuality of bawdy folk tunes and the dreamy eroticism of *bijinga*.

These films are not for viewers who want to see dots connected or tidy resolutions. They are not to be decoded but sunk into. In his book *Poetics of Cinema*, the Chilean filmmaker Raul Ruiz called these kinds of films "poetic objects":

Opposite: *Yumeji*. See page 146.

> The rules you need to understand these poetic objects are unique to each film and must be rediscovered by every viewer; they cannot be described *a priori*, nor *a posteriori* for that matter. In short, these are films that cannot respond to the question, "What is this movie about?" The great French film critic Serge Daney used to distinguish such one-of-a-kind films from the slave products of industry by invoking the difference between true travel and the package tour. In true travel, what matters are the magical accidents, the discoveries, the inexplicable wonders and the wasted time. In a package tour, the pleasure comes from sadistic adherence to a program.[176]

Rayns is one of the few Western writers who have tried to grapple with these particular poetic objects. As he pointed out, "It's necessary to distinguish between Suzuki's insistence on the irrational and the pervasive mystification that still clouds much western perception of Japanese movies and popular art in general."[177] When confronted with something confusing or weird in a foreign film, Western viewers are often quick to chalk it up to an inherent element of the filmmaker's culture that they, as foreigners, can't grasp. But these inscrutable things could just as easily have come from the director's eccentricity or intent to leave questions unanswered.

This mystification is especially complicated in a culture such as Japan's, which is so ancient and complex that the generalist can never expect to get a handle on it.

This mystification is especially complicated in a culture such as Japan's, which is so ancient and complex that the generalist can never expect to get a handle on it. To truly understand any particular element of Japanese culture, one must be a specialist. But you could throw an army of specialists at the Taisho films and still not get to the bottom of them. They can't be unraveled by picking through all the threads of Taisho culture, Japanese folklore, references to art and theater, or analysis of their source materials, because these elements are combined with elements from Suzuki's eccentric imagination.

ZIGEUNERWEISEN

Part of the way through *Zigeunerweisen*, a man and woman begin an affair when she licks his eyeball with the tip of her outstretched tongue to remove a bit of dust (fig. 90). That moment—at once erotic, uncanny, and squirm-inducing—sums up the atmosphere of the trilogy as a whole. At one point during the filming, Toshiya Fujita—a noted director in his own right, who plays one of the film's main roles—was confused about how to play a scene

Fig. 90 *Zigeurnerweisen*

and queried Suzuki about it. According to Ayako Uchida, the film's script supervisor, the conversation got more and more heated until an exasperated Suzuki told Fujita that the key to the movie was that every character was actually dead. This resulted in the cast and crew joking around and pretending to be ghosts for the next few days, causing Suzuki to regret breaking his policy of withholding key information[178]—a habit that bothered Fujita, who, according to Suzuki, said, "Suzuki is sly; he just starts filming without first explaining the situation."[179]

According to Tadao Sato, who heard the story later, Suzuki told Fujita that all the living characters were actually dead and all the dead ones were actually alive.[180] I emphasize the discrepancy between Uchida and Sato's recollections not to point out the faultiness of memory, but because *Zigeunerweisen* is the kind of movie in which either or neither could be true.

The film got its title from a 78 rpm record of a piece of violin music played by Pablo de Sarasate.[181] The recording obsesses Aochi (Fujita), a professor of German, because at one point Sarasate's voice can be heard saying something faintly in the background.

Aochi and his friend and former colleague Nakasago (Yoshio Harada) embody the forces pulling against each other during the Taisho era. The uptight, rational Aochi dresses in Western-style clothes and sports a neatly trimmed mustache. Long-haired, bearded Nakasago dresses in traditional Japanese cloth-

Fig. 91 *Zigeurnerweisen*

ing, and with his perversions, decadence, and death-obsession, he seems to be consciously channeling the primal, untamed urges that Aochi has suppressed in himself. Nakasago flits in and out of the movie, at one point claiming to have murdered a lover, at another returning home with a case of smallpox that infects and kills his wife; he then hires for their child a nurse named O-Ine, who looks exactly like his departed wife and is played by the same actress, Naoko Otani. At another point, Nakasago may be sleeping with Aochi's wife, Taeko (Kisako Makishi). Obsessed with rot and decay, he convinces Aochi to agree that whichever of them dies first, the other will keep his bones.

These elements of the plot become unglued as the movie progresses. Identities shift, and motifs float free from their contexts. We're never sure, for instance, who O-Ine really is, or whether Nakasago actually seduced Taeko—an idea that may have presented itself in a dream to either Aochi or Taeko's bedridden sister, who claims that Aochi "stole" the dream from her. Sarasate's voice even manages to float free of the recording: Taeko is shocked to hear it during lunch in a restaurant. The line "bones pink like cherry blossoms" recurs like a refrain, emphasizing Suzuki's view that cherry blossoms symbolize death, decay, and nihilism.[182] Nakasago's obsession with decay and death—and his own death in the film, which is symbolized by an image of him, now clean-shaven, buried up to his neck in a cherry tree grove—embodies Suzuki's dark interpretation of this traditional symbol (fig. 91).

Fig. 92 *Zigeurnerweisen*

The film's artful elegance is frequently disrupted with jarring effects from Suzuki's B movie repertoire. There are freeze frames and slow-motion tableaus interrupted by quick cuts. Shots often fragment and obscure the logic of the space they are meant to depict. A clumsy special effect of a superimposed crab zooms out of the body of a drowned woman. There is a nod to *Kanto Wanderer*'s famous invisible floor scene when a glass surface appears under Nakasago's feet, with women's faces smashed against it, perhaps representing the many he's victimized (fig. 92).

During a phone conversation between Aochi and Taeko, who are supposedly in separate places, they are shown sitting in the same living room, the camera whip-panning between them as they talk. The news Taeko is delivering—that Nakasago has died of a drug overdose—is accompanied by cherry blossom petals blowing through the open window (fig. 93, fig. 94). This collapse of structural logic turns out to be a rather potent and appropriate move in a film in which one is never sure who is dead or alive, and in which characters continually cross back

Left: Fig. 93 *Zigeurnerweisen*: In this and fig. 94, both characters are in the same room.

Below: Fig. 94 *Zigeurnerweisen*

Fig. 95 *Zigeurnerweisen:* O-Ine in a shot resembling traditional bijinga ghosts.

Fig. 96 *The Ghost of Okiku at Sarayashiki, from the series New Forms of Thirty-six Ghosts*; Tsukioka Yoshitoshi (1839–1892); Japan, Meiji era, 1890; Woodblock print, ink and color on paper; Robert O. Muller Collection; S2003.8.3071. Courtesy of Freer Gallery of Art and Arthur M. Sackler Gallery, Smithsonian Institution.

and forth across the boundary between the two. Toward the end of the film, for instance, O-Ine repeatedly shows up at Aochi and Taeko's house, demanding the mysterious "Zigeunerweisen" recording. Framed against the night sky, her legs obscured,[183] she strongly resembles traditional ghost *bijinga* imagery (fig. 95, fig. 96), causing the viewer to wonder which side of the boundary she is on.

The narrative strands are as fragmented as the shots, as are the relationships between characters. This is a movie filled with lovers' triangles, real and imagined, including one among three blind beggars, a woman and two men, who function as a Greek chorus and comic relief with their bawdy songs and absurd comedy routines (fig. 97). At one point, this group disappears, and Nakasago and O-Ine give Aochi differing accounts of what happened. Nakasago claims the men beat each other to death and the woman drowned. O-Ine says that all three of them married each other. (Both versions of the story are acted out in the style of grotesque burlesque vignettes as they are described.) If there is a key to *Zigeunerweisen*'s mysteries, it may be this exchange: the truth about any of it can never be known.

Fig. 97 The three blind beggars in *Zigeurnerweisen*

KAGERO-ZA

Made one year after *Zigeunerweisen*, *Kagero-za* is adapted from a short novel by the gothic romanticist Izumi Kyoka (1873–1939). The way that motifs, sounds, and lines of dialogue detach from their contexts and float freely through *Zigeunerweisen* continues in *Kagero-za* and is in keeping with the spirit of Kyoka's work. According to Kyoka's translator Charles Shiro Inouye, Kyoka espoused a technique of "'letting go' (*muko makase*)—first harboring some creative notion, then giving free reign to the imagination during the writing process." Inouye could have been writing about Suzuki when he described how Kyoka's short story "One Day in Spring" (which shares motifs with the novel *Kagero-za*) "flood[s] the reader with streams of engaging rhythms and striking images that lead us to the border of transgression and, finally, to an aesthetic epiphany that is more a state of limbo than an increased clarity."[184]

Suzuki admitted to struggling with adapting Kyoka's work to the screen. He said of his source material, "At first I thought the beauty and perfection of the novel would help me in directing the film, but I came to realize that Kyoka's qualities were actually obstacles in my way. A film cannot work if it tries too hard to be beautiful."[185] Suzuki's task was to give cinematic form

Fig. 98 *Kagero-za*: Shinaki walks away...

Fig. 99 ...leaving Matsuzaki alone

Fig. 100 The shot widens to reveal that it is now a point in the future and he is talking to his patron Tamawaki.

to Kyoka's prose, which, though beautiful, contains very little dramatic momentum. He overcame this by creating a structure in which there is fluidity between various narrative layers and within the flow of time. This mutability is announced in an early scene, in which playwright Matsuzaki (Yusaku Matsuda) encounters a mysterious woman named Shinako (Michiyo Okusu). She then leaves the scene and is replaced by Matsuzaki's wealthy patron Tamawaki (Katsuo Nakamura), to whom Matsuzaki describes the encounter. This subtle scene change is actually a shift into the future without warning, which seems to place the viewer in a frame story told by Matsuzaki to Tamawaki. But rather than proceeding into a story-within-a-story, the scene reveals that Shinako is Tamawaki's wife, and that Tamawaki is in the process of stage-managing an affair and love suicide between her and Matsuzaki in the city of Kanazawa (fig. 98, fig. 99, fig. 100).

One thing in Kyoka's novel that interested Suzuki is the idea that "nobody, not even the characters themselves, could imagine that they would commit double-suicide."[186] Tamawaki helps their fate along, and even though Matsuzaki is aware of Tamawaki's plan, he is unable to avoid being drawn into it.

Fig. 101 The blonde, blue-eyed geisha in *Kagero-za*.

None of this is to suggest that the film's plot is in any way straightforward, or that it even matters whether or not Matsuzaki and Shinako actually perish in a double suicide. Matsuzaki's pursuit of Shinako to his possible doom in Kanazawa is the through line that is intersected and interrupted, much like the line between life and death is violated throughout the film. Tamawaki, for instance, has another wife, Ine, who, though Japanese, has blue eyes and blonde hair and seems to move between the living and the dead (fig. 101). Bladder cherries, which, in the film's cosmology, contain the souls of the dead, recur as motifs. On the train to Kanazawa, Matsuzaki runs into an anarchist friend, Wada (Yoshio Harada, in a virtual reprise of his wild-man act in *Zigeunerweisen*), who announces that he wants to blast a hole into the world beyond death so he can have sex with Ine there (he uses a much cruder term). Matsuzaki also encounters a priest who tells him a story about his own son's love suicide, which functions (a bit like the beggar conversation in *Zigeunerweisen*) as a microcosm of Matsuzaki's fate.

Fig. 102 Ekin's paintings decorate the land of the dead in *Kagero-za*.

"Who talks of realism here?" demands a character during the film's ending, which begins as a children's theater performance that morphs into a human puppet theater and then into a performance by Ine from beyond the grave. Eventually, it morphs into an apocalyptic finale in which the plot implodes into the artifice of theater and re-emerges in Suzuki's version of limbo: a land of the dead, where Matsuzaki is surrounded by the grotesque paintings of Ekin, one of Suzuki's favorite painters (fig. 102).

YUMEJI

Unlike the first two films, *Yumeji* isn't based on a previously existing novel, but on an original script by the screenwriter of those films, Yozo Tanaka. It is a freely imagined fictional story inspired by the poet and painter Takehisa Yumeji (1884–1934), a self-taught artist influenced by both Japanese and Western traditions. An outsider to the Japanese art establishment because of his unorthodox style, leftist political leanings, and bohemian lifestyle, he is best known for his *bijinga* paintings and prints of the dreamy, sad-eyed women who served as his mistresses and models. On the occasion of the film's premiere at the Vancouver International Film Festival, Suzuki said,

Yumeji follows its title character as he travels from Tokyo to Kanazawa, where, instead of meeting the woman with whom he plans to elope, he seduces a widow.

"It may not follow the biographical information of the man, and some people may criticize it because of that, but I feel Yumeji was a spontaneous man who did what he wanted. And that's how I approached the film."[187]

Yumeji follows its title character as he travels from Tokyo to Kanazawa,[188] where, instead of meeting the woman with whom he plans to elope, he seduces a widow. She is in search of the body of her husband, whose ghost challenges Yumeji to a duel. The film is as freewheeling in its style, composed of jarring juxtapositions and illogical cuts, as in its narrative. Its declamatory acting bears a distinct Kabuki influence, and much of its visual imagery pushes the earthy eroticism and refined beauty of Yumeji's paintings to more explicit extremes. The seductions, sexual encounters, and general messiness of relationships that lie behind these calm depictions of doe-eyed beauties (see fig. 86) are brought forward. Tomoko Mariya, who plays Yumeji's main muse in the film, bears an almost uncanny resemblance to a model who appears frequently in Yumeji's actual paintings (fig. 103).

Fig. 103 *Yumeji*

As in the other Taisho Trilogy films, *Yumeji*'s plot fragments as it moves from relative reality into a realm between the living and the dead. In its finale, as Yumeji rushes to complete a commission (an obscene painting titled *Song of the Evening Primrose*[189]), the swirling chaos of seductions, betrayals, jealousy, and murder distills into a very Kabuki-like scene. Yumeji confronts multiple versions of himself ushered in by visible stagehands (fig. 104), and the real faces of a bevy of his conquests appear embedded in a painting (fig. 105).

Fig. 104 Yumeji confronts multiple versions of himself.

Fig. 105 *Yumeji*

Even more than *Zigeunerweisen* and *Kagero-za*, *Yumeji* is Suzuki at his most experimental. Logic gives way almost entirely to visual and narrative invention, resulting in a swirl of fragments that only just come into focus as a unified work.

TAISHO TRILOGY AESTHETICS

No longer the studio hand of his Nikkatsu days, Suzuki became, with the Taisho Trilogy, a filmmaker who was taken seriously as an artist, no matter how ambivalent he may be about the idea. Shedding the demands of genre filmmaking led not to the self-indulgence Buruma suggested, but to the freedom to truly merge traditional Japanese aesthetics (albeit of the unruly variety) with film form.

It's interesting to note that this transformation occurred with films set in a time when artists—Yumeji included—began to evolve from hired artisans working for patrons or craftsmen selling decorative items to self-conscious creators expressing their individuality. All three films are obsessed with artistic expression and present it as a kind of supernatural conjuring. The

No longer the studio hand of his Nikkatsu days, Suzuki became, with the Taisho Trilogy, a filmmaker who was taken seriously as an artist, no matter how ambivalent he may be about the idea.

Zigeunerweisen recording, with its ghostly voice, becomes a ghost itself when it floats free from its physical object to surprise Taeko in the restaurant scene; the record becomes an obsession for Nakasago's wife when, after his death, she repeatedly visits Aochi at night—appearing to be an apparition herself—in search of it. The theatrical performance at the end of *Kagero-za* morphs into a confession by Ine from beyond the grave, and Tamawaki's scheme to manipulate Matsuzaki into committing suicide is an extended theatrical endeavor in itself. In the end of that film, everything is reduced to a paper image sinking into the water as Matsuzaki journeys to a land of the dead decorated with Ekin's phantasmagoric paintings. In *Yumeji*, Suzuki finds yet another way to misuse superimpositions, as images of the artist's work appear on a pillar whenever he touches it (fig. 106, fig. 107). And by divorcing *Yumeji* from the biographical facts, Suzuki creates a portrait of an artist whose works come to life to torment him.

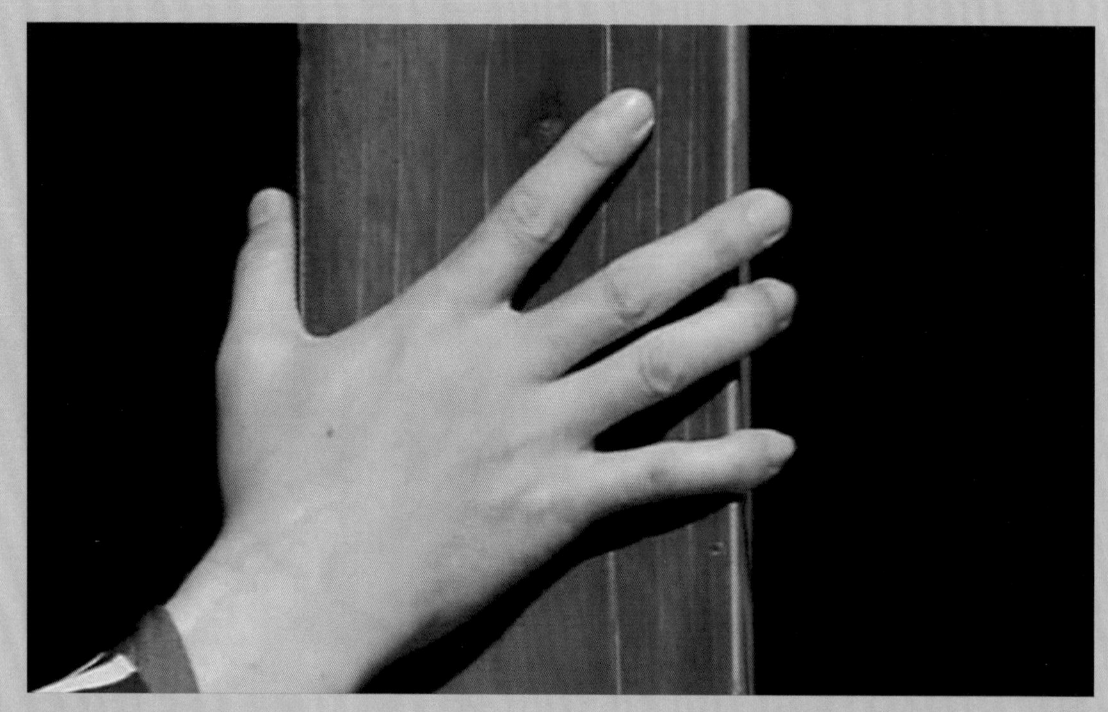

Fig. 106 Yumeji's hand conjures...

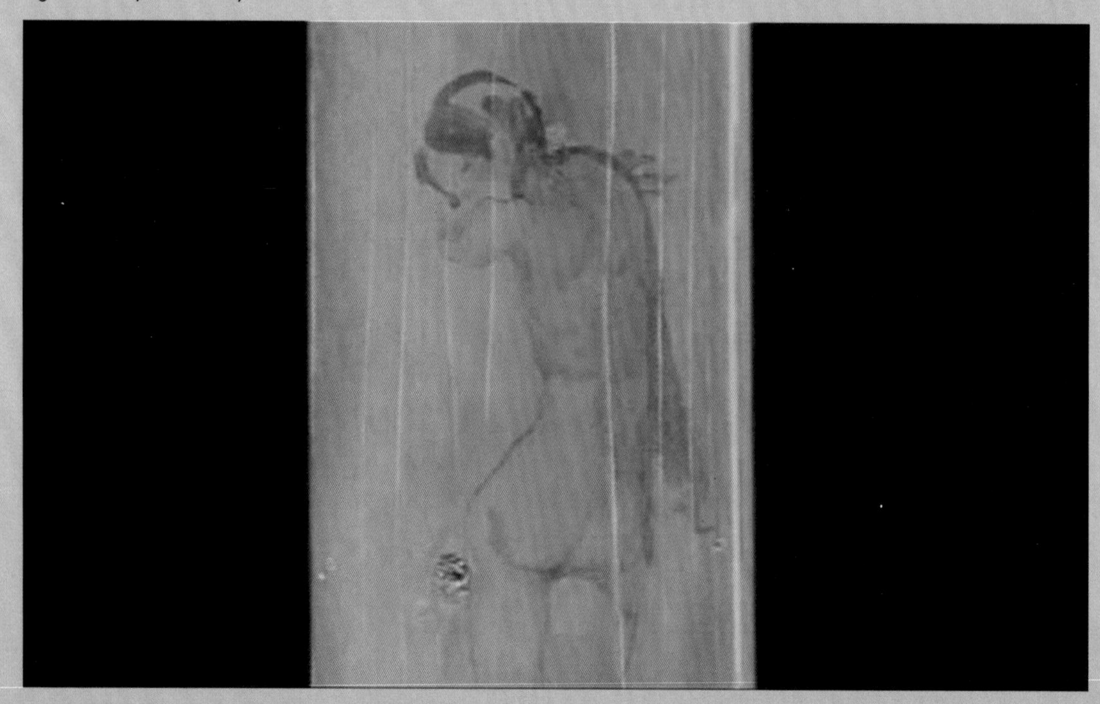

Fig. 107 ...a superimposition of his art on a wooden pillar.

These films are infinitely more open to interpretation than the Nikkatsu films. Even at his most fragmented and freewheeling in *Branded to Kill*, Suzuki tethered his inventiveness to a plot that can be sussed out with a bit of work. The Taisho Trilogy's embrace of ambiguity and refusal to resolve mysteries allies it with the European art cinema of Fellini, Bunuel, Antonioni, and other directors of the era whose films defy rigid interpretation. Such films approach the condition of "open work" as defined by Umberto Eco, in that the viewer must contribute to their meaning through active engagement.

Eco's discussion of Kafka's use of symbolism bears some relation to Suzuki's leap from the concreteness of genre plots to the ambiguity of the Taisho films:

> It is easy to think of Kafka's work as "open": trial, castle, waiting, passing sentence, sickness, metamorphosis, and torture—none of these narrative situations is to be understood in the immediate literal sense. But, unlike the constructions of medieval allegory, where the superimposed layers of meaning are rigidly prescribed, in Kafka there is no confirmation in an encyclopedia, no matching paradigm in the cosmos, to provide a key to the symbolism. The various existentialist, theological, clinical, and psychoanalytic interpretations of Kafka's symbols cannot exhaust all the possibilities of his works. The work remains inexhaustible insofar as it is "open," because in it an ordered world based on universally acknowledged laws is being replaced by a world based on ambiguity, both in the negative sense that directional centers are missing and in a positive sense, because values and dogma are constantly being placed in question.[190]

As with Kafka's inexhaustible symbols, there is no definitive answer, in the Taisho films, as to who is dead and who is alive, what was a dream and what wasn't, or whether there is a hidden meaning behind any particularly strange image. Open works acknowledge the contribution of the audience, encourage repeated viewings that yield new interpretations, and sometimes force re-evaluation in light of ambiguous or unexpected endings.[191]

For better or worse, fans of Suzuki's Nikkatsu films include many who are quick to apply the dismissive epithet "arty" to anything with ambitions beyond the slam-bang pleasures of genre cinema. This is a major reason why the Taisho Trilogy films remain so underappreciated outside of Japan. For his fans, it was almost like the Taisho films were made by a different director.

In searching for points of comparison, many people saw similarities between the Taisho films and those of Federico Fellini, with their surreal images and dream logic. The comparison seems to have irked Suzuki considerably. In a rambling 1980 essay called "Random Notes on Fellini (or: I don't like it)," he made his position clear:

> When I was doing a campaign for my next but last picture, people who had seen it asked me if I had been influenced by Fellini. I could hardly suppress my anger, although I have completely forgotten his films. Nothing is more difficult than making films under the influence of someone else. ... It's possible to draw comparisons, but for the person who is compared with someone else, this is unbearable. ... The questions they ask you on these occasions fall just short of insults; such and such a scene does resemble such a scene in Fellini's film rather a lot, and I'm only guessing here, but I think that Fellini worked according to such and such a concept, so what is your concept? Everyone who is interested in film says that Fellini is an interesting director. I don't want to argue with this, but to an uneducated man like me it's practically impossible to understand what's so interesting about Fellini.[192]

While Suzuki was toiling away at Nikkatsu in the 1960s, a self-conscious art cinema, made by directors who embraced their status as artists, was emerging in Europe. By the time Suzuki made the Taisho films, this type of filmmaking had become familiar to cinephiles and critics as the default house style of serious film festivals. If, in this context, Suzuki's Taisho films came across as "bad fake Fellini," it is because Suzuki always kept one foot in the genre camp, peppering his version of art films with trashy effects from his Nikkatsu arsenal. This suggests to some that he wasn't actually capable of making serious films, but I'm sure I'm not alone in thinking that this deliberate vulgarity makes these films distinctive. In their mix of seriousness and silliness, almost superstitious treatment of artistic creation, and refusal to surrender their secrets to analysis, the Taisho films epitomize Suzuki's lifelong balancing act between taking nothing seriously and creating ambitious works that ask to be.

The Taisho films reside in liminal spaces between dreams and reality, and between art and entertainment—hence their resistance to interpretation, except as expressions of the irrationality Suzuki thought cinema needed more of. He once said in an interview, "I don't really feel there is any irrationality nowadays. I think that's bad. The problem is that there's no balance between rationalism and irrationality, and that leads to madness. That's why I think that the irrational, which has always existed, should be brought out more in films."[193] ●

175 Tony Rayns, "*Yumeji*," in *Branded to Thrill: The Delirious Cinema of Suzuki Seijun* (London: British Film Institute, 1995), 45.

176 Raul Ruiz, *Poetics of Cinema* (Paris: Editions Dis Voir, 1995), 77–78.

177 Rayns, "The Kyoka Factor," 8.

178 Uchida, interview.

179 Suzuki and Ueno, "Forgetting Foreign Names," 74.

180 Sato, interview.

181 Rayns, "*Zigeunerweisen*," in *Branded to Thrill: The Delirious Cinema of Suzuki Seijun* (London: British Film Institute, 1995), 43.

182 In his self-interview, Suzuki remembered a novel that describes "how a cherry tree flowers more richly and beautifully than before because it extracts nourishment from a dead body buried under it. ... To my mind, no other flower symbolizes death and dying than the cherry blossom, because mortality and nihilism loom behind its beauty." Suzuki, "The Desert under the Cherry Tree," 58.

183 In Japanese folklore, ghosts are always depicted without legs.

184 Charles Shiro Inouye, "Essays," in *In Light of Shadows: More Gothic Tales by Izumi Kyoka* (Honolulu: University of Hawaii Press, 2005), 176.

185 Suzuki, "Suzuki on Suzuki," 29.

186 Ibid.

187 Monk, "Japanese legend sees himself as simple chronicler."

188 Some commentators, most notably Rayns, have surmised that Kanazawa holds some mystical meaning to Suzuki. When I asked Suzuki about it, he responded that it didn't mean much to him at all. Suzuki, email to the author (translated by Yuka Sakano), February 19, 2014.

189 This is also the title of a poem that the real Yumeji wrote, which became a popular song.

190 Umberto Eco, *The Open Work* (Cambridge: Harvard University Press, 1989), 6.

191 A recent example is Nuri Bilge Ceylon's *Once Upon a Time in Anatolia* (2011), which takes the form of a murder mystery until the last scene, in which it's revealed to be about something else entirely.

192 Suzuki, "Random Notes on Fellini," 52.

193 Suzuki et al., "The Tiger and the Messenger," 63.

12

LATE RECOGNITION

IN 1994, *Branded to Thrill: The Delirious Cinema of Suzuki Seijun*, a retrospective comprising a selection of the Nikkatsu films and the entire Taisho Trilogy, commenced a tour throughout Europe and North America. Several of these fourteen films were subsequently released on DVD in those regions, accompanied by interviews with Suzuki, Kimura, and Shishido, in which these three old timers seem genuinely thrilled at the attention. In the wake of this late recognition, Suzuki entered yet another phase of his career. *Pistol Opera* (2001) and *Princess Raccoon* (2005) incorporate stylistic elements from both his Nikkatsu and Taisho films, while making use of technological advances that had occurred in the interim.

PISTOL OPERA

Suzuki's return to filmmaking after a second ten-year hiatus was occasioned by producer Satoru Ogura, who approached him about making a sequel to *Branded to Kill*. The result was *Pistol Opera* (2001), which is not so much a sequel as a compact retrospective of Suzuki's style and themes. Makiko Esumi plays Stray Cat who, like Jo Shishido's character in *Branded*, must battle her way to the top of the pecking order of assassins in her organization. The film's structure, which consists of set piece after set piece with little connective tissue, and the ritualized dance or mime-like movements of the actors mix a Nikkatsu-style potboiler plot with the through-and-through inventiveness of the Taisho films.

There are references sprinkled throughout to not only *Branded* but other films from his career. Mikijiro Hira make an appearance playing Shishido's character from *Branded* thirty years on.[194] Stray Cat silhouetted before a shoji screen (fig. 108) recalls the famous fight scene in *Tattooed Life*. One scene reprises Okaru's mirror trick from *Kanto Wanderer* (Stray Cat uses the mirror

Fig. 108 *Pistol Opera*

to aim her gun at a rival). A shot of a backhoe dumping a load of flower petals recalls the dialectic between hard and soft surfaces in *Underworld Beauty*.

Like the Taisho Trilogy, *Pistol Opera* evidences Suzuki's preoccupation with the idea of fluidity between the living and the dead. As in *Zigeunerweisen*, a spooky child seems to straddle those worlds. Stray Cat repeatedly finds herself in a yellow-tinted land of the dead where she is often on a boat or dock (bringing to mind the River Styx), with her victims appearing like ghosts around her. Unlike the earthbound Hanada in *Branded*, Stray Cat journeys to metaphysical realms, haunted by the death she deals and constantly reminded that it is also in store for her.

With the nonsensical elements of his films finally being celebrated as strengths, Suzuki gave the people the absurdity they wanted in *Pistol Opera*. Time and space have little unity; with no transition, characters move from a country house, say, to an industrial wasteland. One rival assassin is an American cowboy who can feel no pain and is dispatched when Stray Cat

With the nonsensical elements of his films finally being celebrated as strengths, Suzuki gave the people the absurdity they wanted in *Pistol Opera*.

fools him into stabbing himself in the heart. Another killer sports a blond hairdo, sniffles constantly, and specializes in shooting his victims in a precise spot in the neck that leaves a smiling corpse. One character delivers a monologue about Japan's first color movie, Keisuke Kinoshita's *Carmen Comes Home* (1951), recalling scenes of burning flags and mud that appear nowhere in the actual film.[195] The "Terror Expo" where the climax takes place is a crazy mix of *butoh* dancers, cherry blossoms, Roman columns, and paintings of atrocities by Goya and others (fig. 109).

As if to further confuse those seeking symbolism in Suzuki's use of color, yellow here clearly represents death (as opposed to the "niceness and compromise" he once claimed it did). Yellow light suffuses the land of the dead that Stray Cat visits more than once (fig. 110). Upon one character's death, a yellow mist appears, and another character meets death while wearing a yellow kimono. Overall, the colors are dazzling and garish, and their effect is heightened by the film's anachronistic, nearly square 1.33:1 aspect ratio[196] and the use of CGI in some scenes.

Fig. 109 *Pistol Opera*

Fig. 110 *Pistol Opera*'s yellow-tinged land of the dead.

Princess Raccoon, which followed four years later, uses CGI much more thoroughly, enabling Suzuki to reach new heights of artificiality. A musical fairy tale inspired by Keigo Kimura's musicals of the 1940s and '50s, the film was one Suzuki had been thinking about making for some twenty years. A prince (Jo Odagiri) is banished to a mysterious mountain populated by shape-shifting raccoon demons[197] and falls in forbidden love with their princess (Zhang Ziyi). The general setting is an imaginary Edo period composed of a strange mix of theater-like sets and digital manipulations, accompanied by anachronistic songs ranging from operetta to hip-hop to a pop song about soda. Edo-style paintings come to life through computer animation; fittingly,

Fig. 111 Princess Raccoon emerges from a Chinese landscape painting.

since she is Chinese, Zhang emerges from an animated Chinese-style painting (fig. 111). The prince's journey to the mountain is illustrated using an Edo-era screen painting, also fitting because narrative paintings of that time use cinema-like effects to tell their stories (chief among them being the use of painted clouds as "fades" between scenes).

Fig. 112 *Princess Raccoon*'s kabuki fight in the "dark."

Fig. 113 *Princess Raccoon*

Scenes that aren't digitally enhanced have a deliberately stage-like quality, using minimal decor, bare sets, and artificial colors. There is a Kabuki-like fight scene in the "dark" (fig. 112) and a Kabuki-style staging of a death scene near the end that echoes the finale of Shakespeare's *Romeo and Juliet* (fig. 113). Set designer Takeo Kimura had been working with Suzuki for more than forty

Fig. 114 *Princess Raccoon*

Fig. 115 *Princess Raccoon*

years at that point, and the sets in *Pistol Opera* are a return to the bare-bones, dime-store inventiveness of those for such films as *Gate of Flesh* and *Tokyo Drifter*. In one scene, Odagiri's Prince Amechiyo wanders onto an empty, stage-like set while the lights change color to indicate extreme heat changing to extreme cold, with both the forms of the set and the use of overall light changes echoing *Drifter*'s grand finale so closely that it might be a deliberate reference (fig. 114, fig. 115). Toward the end, characters who have died appear resurrected under a cherry tree, making me wonder if Suzuki's attitude toward what he has described as a symbol of death and battle had changed. Rather than fertilizing the tree with their corpses, these figures achieve new life as they emerge beneath it (fig. 116).

Fig. 116 *Princess Raccoon*: Resurrection under the cherry tree.

In differing ways, *Pistol Opera* and *Princess Raccoon* look back on Suzuki's long career from the perspective of old age. With their careers subject to the vagaries of film production, this is a privilege relatively few other filmmakers are able to enjoy. Some directors, unable to secure financing, make their final films at an early age. Others, such as George Cukor, maintain a similar style even as they work into old age. John Ford's late films have an air of solemn wisdom about them. The last films of Manoel de Oliveira, who made his final film in 2014 and died at the age of 106 in 2015, often take an amused, indulgent attitude toward human foibles that comes with age and experience. Although Suzuki was pitching a new project as late as 2008, the year he turned eighty-five,[198] *Princess Raccoon* is almost certainly his final film. There's an easygoing spirit to it, especially in its final musical number, which breaks the fourth wall and addresses the audience directly. It's a movie that, in effect, says goodbye at the end (fig. 117). ●

Fig. 117 *Princess Raccoon*

194 When he mentions to Stray Cat that the original assassins list was made after the Tokyo Olympics, it dovetails nicely (if perhaps inadvertently) with Daisuke Miyao's analysis of *Branded* as a commentary on the changes the Olympics brought to the Tokyo cityscape.

195 This marks the second reference in Suzuki's oeuvre to *Carmen Comes Home*, the first being *Carmen from Kawachi*. When I asked him about it, he simply said he appreciates it for its cheerfulness and lightness. Seijun Suzuki, email to the author (translated by Yuka Sakano), June 9, 2014.

196 Suzuki credited this idea to cinematographer Yonezo Maeda, who "felt that in this format every part of the screen would be equally dense with colour." Mes, "Japan Cult Cinema Interview: Seijun Suzuki."

197 In Japanese, the creatures are *tanuki*—raccoon-like dogs native to Japan, whose reputation as shape-shifters in Japanese folklore dates back to at least the 8th century BCE.

198 Kimura entered the Guinness Book of World Records the same year, when he made his directorial debut at age 90.

13

SUZUKI'S IMPACT AND INFLUENCE

In Japan, Suzuki has been a public figure and his films have remained in circulation since the 1960s. Consciousness of his work elsewhere emerged later, through his influence on younger filmmakers and shifts in public taste toward the kind of genre experimentation he pioneered.

SUZUKI'S INFLUENCE IN JAPAN

Made famous by his battle with Nikkatsu, Suzuki maintained his celebrity status in Japan even when he wasn't creating films, through his books and appearances on television and in other directors' movies. His Nikkatsu films remained popular with cinephiles long after they were made. (He was even named Japan's best-dressed man in 1985 by the Japanese Fashion Society.) Suzuki's 1990s resurgence made him cool for a whole new generation of Japanese filmmakers who absorbed his anarchic aesthetics and sometimes paid tribute by casting him in their films. Shinji Aoyama, who gave Suzuki a role in his darkly comic horror movie *EM: Embalming* (1999), explained Suzuki's appeal to his generation:

> What Suzuki represents to me is anarchy. He's a complete anarchist, and he's the only person in Japanese cinema who could get away with a film like *A Tale of Sorrow and Sadness.* I was born in 1964 and so I was in my early teens when I experienced punk, and on me Jean-Luc Godard and Seijun Suzuki had the same sort of impact.[199]

Suzuki's former assistant Kensaku Watanabe cast him in his movie *The Story of Pu Pu* in 1998; another young director, Sabu, cast him in *Blessing Bell* (2002). The blends of violence, kitsch, and dark humor in these films distinctly reflect their Suzuki influence. Indeed, so pervasive is his influence

Opposite: *Ghost Dog: The Way of the Samurai*. See page 165.

on younger Japanese filmmakers that, as Mark Schilling wrote, "many young Japanese directors are also far more Suzukiesque than they are Ozuesque or Oshimaesque, even if they have seen none of Suzuki's films. He doesn't tower as a sui generis genius so much as he infiltrates and insinuates."[200] A direct line can be traced from Suzuki to contemporary Japanese filmmakers such as Aoyama, Takashi Miike, and Sion Sono, whose films' gory violence and sexual perversity mix with humor and stylistic flamboyance. That these directors' works regularly screen at prestigious international film festivals in Cannes, Berlin, Toronto, and elsewhere is an indication of how much this kind of filmmaking has been accepted as a serious form of cinematic art.

A FILMMAKERS' FILMMAKER

Consciousness of Suzuki's work in the West was first filtered through the films of directors who were directly influenced by him, or who shared his taste for stylized violence or parodying genre cinema. These practices were becoming popular around the time Suzuki's films made their way into Western theaters and video stores.

Suzuki's 1990s traveling retrospective was the first occasion for many in the West to see his films. By the time it started circulating among cities in Europe and America, the films of John Woo and other Hong Kong directors, which revived the gangster movie genre as a new kind of kinetic pop art, had begun attracting legions of American devotees. One vocal champion of those films, Quentin Tarantino, had already caused pop culture sensations with *Reservoir Dogs* (1992) and *Pulp Fiction* (1994), both for their then-shocking amounts of violence and for Tarantino's sincere connoisseurship of trashy B movie aesthetics. Thanks to him and his many followers, formerly dismissed genres such as kung fu movies, gangster flicks, and blacksploitation films, along with the kinds of B movies Suzuki made, gained a new cultural caché.

Like Suzuki, Woo understood that genre movies should be exercises in style, the more flamboyant the better. In *A Better Tomorrow* (1986), a swaggering Chow Yun-fat lights a cigarette with a hundred dollar bill. In *The Killer* (1989), bullets rain down in slow motion in a gunfight, and two armed rivals comically pretend they are having tea with the blind woman whose apartment they've invaded. In 2012, Woo signaled his admiration of Suzuki by announcing plans to direct a remake of *Youth of the Beast*, though the project remains unrealized as of this writing.[201] The kineticism of Woo's films comes from the constant movement between tension and release, a technique Tarantino absorbed and took to extremes by stretching the tension

Fig. 118 *Ghost Dog: The Way of the Samurai.* (Compare with fig. 49, page 61.)

for as long as possible and making the release as violent as possible. (Think of the ear-slicing scene in *Reservoir Dogs* or Samuel L. Jackson's pre-massacre biblical speech in *Pulp Fiction.*)

Directors such as Woo and Tarantino take genre conventions seriously enough to play with them, foregrounding form and style over substance. When Tarantino, Jim Jarmusch, and other filmmakers began to champion his work, Suzuki's stature in cinema (at least in the United States) could be likened to the Velvet Underground's in pop music during the 1960s. Brian Eno famously said[202] that the Velvet Underground may have only sold 30,000 albums in the early years, but "everyone who bought one of those 30,000 copies started a band."

Like the bands inspired by the Velvet Underground's blend of pop and experimentation, filmmakers paid homage to those elements in Suzuki's work. Jarmusch's *Ghost Dog: The Way of the Samurai* (1999) is a loose remake of Suzuki's *Branded to Kill* that includes a scene lifted directly from it: the brilliant bit of absurdity in which an assassin kills a guy bending over his bathroom sink by firing a bullet through the plumbing in the basement (fig. 118). Jarmusch made no attempt to hide the fact that he stole from Suzuki. Rather, he drew attention to Suzuki while publicizing his own film, and even showed it to Suzuki in order to get his opinion.[203] Among the some twenty references[204] to Japanese movies in Tarantino's *Kill Bill Vol. 1* (2003) is a

Fig. 119 *Kill Bill Vol. 1*

nod to the see-through floor shots in *Tattooed Life* (fig. 119). Baz Luhrmann, another devotee of stylistic flourishes and bold colors, described Suzuki as "a director who seemed to have known the future before it happened."

Wong Kar-wai's films bear a clear Suzuki influence in their daring use of saturated colors, stylized energy, and off-kilter compositions (fig. 120) as well as Wong's improvisatory directing technique, for which he is even more notorious than Suzuki is. His films are under constant revision during production: "He has no finished script when he begins shooting. He arrives at the set early and decides on the camera positions, then gives actors their dialogue, which he has usually composed a few hours before."[205] Wong also used soundtrack music from *Yumeji* in his own *In the Mood for Love* (2000), and I suspect that the canned pineapples that one character ritualistically eats in *Chungking Express* (1994) are a reference to Suzuki's *Gate of Flesh*, in which the canned fruit figures prominently as scavenged foodstuffs that the characters gobble down.

Just as there are writers' writers and musicians' musicians, Suzuki is a filmmakers' filmmaker. This is why directors as different as Baz Luhrmann and Jim Jarmusch both sing his praises. Craftspeople themselves, they recognize that his innovations are on the level of craft and form. Directors are steeped in the rules of narrative filmmaking. The thrill for them is in watching Suzuki flagrantly break those rules when he inserts an invisible floor into a scene or makes a hash out of a script's plot in order to emphasize its nonsensicalness. This is the kind of "total anarchy" Aoyama referred to. It is precisely the violations of the rules that got him fired from Nikkatsu that are most appreciated—especially by other filmmakers—in his work today.

As Steve Rose put it in *The Guardian*, "Given the number and spread of [Suzuki's] disciples, you could be forgiven for wondering if his omission from the history books wasn't part of some odd conspiracy."[206] The real reasons are more mundane. The most obvious is that his work wasn't known outside of Japan when the first major English-language histories of Japanese cinema were written, and when he was finally discovered, he didn't fit into the standard narrative of masters and masterpieces those histories usually follow. Whether it's a question of access or taste, the hundreds of B movies produced by Nikkatsu, Shintoho, and other studios weren't taken seriously enough to be included. To his credit, Donald Richie did attempt to right this wrong with his 2001 book *A Hundred Years of Japanese Cinema*, which includes Suzuki and attempts to look at Japanese film more broadly, including B movies and other

Fig. 120 Wong Kar-wai's *2046*

genres not previously considered important. (He didn't mention Suzuki's post-Nikkatsu films, however.) Simply put, Suzuki is an anomaly, and those are hard to shoehorn into historical narratives. Instead, he became the property of cult film aficionados, profiled alongside other genre heroes in books such as *Outlaw Masters of Japanese Cinema* and *The Yakuza Movie Book*.

So maybe Suzuki is, as he once playfully claimed in an interview, a "prophet"[207] after all. Luhrmann's assertion that he somehow knew the future is echoed by Schilling, who wrote that Suzuki's Nikkatsu films "foretold the course of much of popular culture over the next three decades, both in Japan and the West."[208] As I mentioned previously, what makes *A Tale of Sorrow and Sadness* such a strange viewing experience is that it looks less like a Suzuki film than it does a product of a culture that had completely absorbed his bizarre aesthetics.

AN AUDIENCE PRIMED FOR VIOLENCE AND IRONY

One of the reasons films such as *Tokyo Drifter* and *Branded to Kill* retain their appeal is that their campy, ironic handling of genre material feels more at home in the pop culture landscape of the 1990s through today than in the 1960s. When Suzuki's films began appearing on movie screens and home video in the West, irony, camp, and winking self-awareness had become mainstream methods for approaching genre filmmaking. John Waters embraced this mode in his underground films of the 1970s and '80s, such as *Pink Flamingoes* (1972) and *Female Trouble* (1974), but by 1994 he was achieving broad popular success with films such as *Hairspray* (1988), *Cry-Baby* (1990), and *Serial Mom* (1994). These films dispensed with the explicitness and gross-out scenes that made his earlier films so notorious, but they retain the campy, loving attitude toward trash. Similarly, Sam Raimi's *The Evil Dead* (1981), which played at the Cannes Film Festival and spawned two hit sequels, affectionately pokes fun at horror movie tropes while reveling in them. Fans of Tarantino, Waters, and Raimi were well primed for Suzuki's knowing violations of B movie norms.

Suzuki's anarchic exploding of tropes and conventions was the result of him hitting the limits of genre. After spending so many years trying to make unique films out of the same material, he became unable to take them seriously. He pushed his narratives ever closer to nonsense, deploying humor that depends on his audiences' familiarity with the clichés he was sending up in the late Nikkatsu films. What Nikkatsu boss Hori found "incomprehensible" in *Tokyo Drifter* or *Branded to Kill* would have been entirely comprehensible to the members of the Cine Clubs, who had seen enough Nikkatsu Action movies to know that Suzuki was deliberately making fun of their conventions.

The Cine Clubs may have been a niche audience of serious cinephiles, but decades later ironic detachment and parody in genre filmmaking hit the mainstream. The rise of home video made it possible to see so many films that use the same worn-out conventions that it became impossible to approach them with a straight face. Filmmakers of this later generation, who themselves grew up binging on genre movies, made this knowingly satirical and ironic approach to genre one of its default modes. As a recent example, the comedy in *The Cabin in the Woods* (Drew Goddard, 2012) depends on its audience being familiar with the clichés of the horror genre. Its opening scenes of sex-crazed college kids taking off to a spooky old house for the weekend deliberately evoke any number of slasher movies from the 1970s until today. The subsequent jokes and plot twists all hinge on viewers' assumed familiarity with the standard plots of those films.

It is in this satirical register that Suzuki's work resonates perhaps even more pervasively with audiences today than it does on a formal level. You can sense Suzuki's influence on the high-priced pulp of the *Fast and Furious* franchise, for instance. With each installment, the car chases become more detached from reality and the laws of physics. Watching the trailer for the latest edition, *Furious 7* (2015), in which the heroes begin a car chase in the sky, inside cars dangling from parachutes, made me wonder if director James Wan had also reached a height of absurdity in a quest for the pure action film.

A reader of an early draft of this manuscript accused me of perpetuating the legend that Suzuki was a lone artist toiling among hacks at Nikkatsu. I'll admit that I stewed over this remark on my way to show *Tokyo Drifter* to a group of college students—Asian studies majors, for the most part, who had little or no familiarity with his work and were born some three decades after *Drifter* was released. Their enthusiastic, knowing laughter at the film's over-the-top violations of action movie tropes confirmed for me part of what distinguishes Suzuki from his contemporaries. He was the only one to take

In addition to appreciating irony and generic parody, audiences today have a much higher tolerance for sex and violence than they did in 1988, when the Edinburgh Film Festival felt the need to warn its audience about those elements in Suzuki's films.

such a knowingly ironic and campy approach to his material, which, considering how pop culture evolved in the decades after *Drifter* was made, really does appear to be ahead of its time.

In addition to appreciating irony and generic parody, audiences today have a much higher tolerance for sex and violence than they did in 1988, when the Edinburgh Film Festival felt the need to warn its audience about those elements in Suzuki's films. In that warning, Paul Willemen included a statement made by Ian Buruma: "In Japan even the most horrifying violence, as long as it is not real, can be judged purely aesthetically."[209] I am generally wary of Westerners explaining Asian sensibilities in broad strokes, but if this aestheticizing of violence is somehow an intrinsically Japanese trait, a version of it pervades American genre movies today. Directors such as Tarantino, Robert Rodriguez, Eli Roth, and others take an ironic approach to genre that allows them to present violence—even sexual violence—in such a distanced way as to make it a purely aesthetic spectacle. It becomes a game of seeing how extreme things can get, which the audience, in on the joke, can watch in a similarly distanced way. In Tarantino's *Death Proof* (2007), when a car tire runs over a woman's face, leaving its imprint on her crushed skull, the intent seems to be to provoke shocked laughter, not sadness over the character's death or offense at the scene's gratuitousness. I point this out not to condemn gratuitous violence, but to note that gratuitousness ceases to be a category when stylized violence is meant to be appreciated for its aesthetic qualities (however gruesome they may be). For better or worse, the pop culture landscape these filmmakers have produced over the last two decades is one reason why even young audiences appreciate the stylized, comedic violence in Suzuki's Nikkatsu films. ●

199 Tom Mes and Jasper Sharp, *The Midnight Eye Guide to Japanese Film* (Berkeley: Stone Bridge Press, 2005), 3.

200 Schilling, *The Yakuza Movie Book*, 96.

201 Pamela McClintock, "Cannes 2012: John Woo Set to Remake Classic Japanese Mafia Pic 'Youth of the Beast,'" accessed April 21, 2015, http://www.hollywoodreporter.com/news/cannes-john-woo-youth-of-beast-325524

202 Kristine McKenna, "Eno: Voyages in Time & Perception," *Musician*, accessed April 21, 2015, http://music.hyperreal.org/artists/brian_eno/interviews/musn82.htm

203 Robert Wilonsky, "The Way of Jim Jarmusch," *Miami New Times*, accessed April 21, 2015, http://www.miaminewtimes.com/film/the-way-of-jim-jarmusch-6356787

204 The Quentin Tarantino Archives, "*Kill Bill* References Guide," accessed May 12, 2015, http://wiki.tarantino.info/index.php/Kill_Bill_References_Guide/japanese#Tokyo_Drifter_.281966.29

205 David Bordwell, *Planet Hong Kong: Popular Cinema and the Art of Entertainment* (Cambridge: Harvard University Press, 2000), 271.

206 Steve Rose, "Man on the Moon," *The Guardian*, accessed May 12, 2015, http://www.theguardian.com/film/2006/jun/30/1

207 Monk, "Japanese legend sees himself as simple chronicler."

208 Schilling, *The Yakuza Movie Book*, 95.

209 Suzuki, Willemen, and Sato, *The Films of Seijun Suzuki*, 34.

Conclusion

As I was writing this book, I heard an interview with an author[210] who claimed that the idea of sitting in a movie theater for two hours has become so old-fashioned as to be laughable—a remnant of the industrial revolution, before radio and television, when workers flocking to big cities needed something to do in the evening. We don't *watch* movies now, he suggested; we *consume* them, in two-minute bursts on our phones or in binge-watching sessions on our couches. As someone whose day job involves trying to get people to watch movies in a theater, I felt a twinge of umbrage at this remark. But, having acquired a bit of Suzuki's genial nihilism as I worked on this project, I can shrug it off, cop to my own possible obsolescence, and admit that there is more than a grain of truth in what he said.

The fact is that, as movie "consumption" has migrated onto television, computer, and phone screens, the cinematheques and repertory theaters that hosted Suzuki's *Branded to Thrill* retrospective twenty years ago hold a less central place in film culture. The influence of critics who promoted his work in film publications has been diluted as film critics and bloggers have proliferated online. More films than ever are available to us, but they can be harder to find due to the fragmented way that information reaches us in the Internet age. In other words, it's hard to imagine Suzuki's work making the same impact today as it did when he was "discovered" in the West in the 1990s.

But this is not necessarily a negative development. With so many films now available to be seen, the arguments over the merits of films and filmmakers once considered too trashy, commercial, or cheap for serious consideration have lost much of their importance. These battles, including Godard and Truffaut pushing for Hollywood directors to be considered artists in the 1950s and Pauline Kael's notorious review defending the excessive violence in Arthur Penn's *Bonnie and Clyde* (1967), stirred such passion because, at the time, a powerful critic's review could make or break a movie's chances for success. Richard Brody pointed this out in a *New Yorker* blog post critiquing the current "vulgar auteurism" movement in film criticism: "This is an age of aesthetic extremes, whether in the demotic blandishments of mass entertainment or the gravity and austerity of the art houses' so-called slow cinema. ... There is now little need to trawl recondite corners for the most unfathomably fantastic aesthetic extremes, because many of them are nearly mainstream, and the mainstream makes room for them as it formerly didn't and couldn't."[211]

In their own way, the "vulgar auteurists" are looking to discover and champion new Seijun Suzukis among the current crop of action and horror movie directors who are regarded by other critics as mere studio hacks. This is, in a way, an admirable endeavor, but if the mainstream can be defined as what is readily available to us, then virtually the entire history of cinema is now part of it. We can all access it easily from our homes, which says to me that the battle they are fighting may have already been fought and won.

Suzuki's films are best appreciated as they were intended to be shown, in a movie theater surrounded by an audience and projected in their original 35mm format, but many of them are part of the capacious mainstream in video form. People continue to discover and be inspired by them online and on DVD, sometimes in ways that are only possible because of the Internet and new technology. In my research, I've stumbled across everything from beautiful little animated gifs made of images from *Branded to Kill* to a 2012 hip-hop song called "Seijun Suzuki" by the Blue Scholars (sampling music from *Tokyo Drifter*), to any number of bloggers who found his films and just had to tell the world about them.

The fact that these tributes exist is inspiring in its own way. They represent a new mode of interacting with movies. Once-passive spectators become participants, creating artworks in response to those they watch. The surface of the screen, which so preoccupied Suzuki throughout his career, has become porous. We can reach in and take what we want. I believe this legendary rule-breaker and affable collaborator would certainly appreciate an audience willing to break the unwritten rules of spectatorship and collaborate with him.

Perhaps the real "Suzuki Seijun Problem" is that he is an artist who refuses to consider himself one. He's always claimed to be merely an entertainer, explaining away anything experimental in his work as just a way to keep things interesting for the audience. But just as artworks sometimes need to be defended against their advocates, sometimes artists have to be defended against themselves. Suzuki's refusal to consider himself an artist is an artistic stance in itself, whether he likes it or not. ●

210 Patrick Tucker, "Predicting the Future with Phone Data and Tweets," *The Kojo Nnamdi Show*, July 8, 2014, radio broadcast, http://thekojonnamdishow.org/shows/2014-07-08/predicting-future-phone-data-and-tweets

211 Richard Brody, "A Few Thoughts on Vulgar Auteurism," *The New Yorker*, accessed May 12, 2015, http://www.newyorker.com/online/blogs/movies/2013/06/vulgar-auteurism-history-of-new-wave-cinema.html

APPENDICES

APPENDIX 1

Filmography with Selected Synopses

Films through 1985 adapted from Koshi Ueno, Suzuki Seijun, zen-eiga (Suzuki Seijun, All his Films), Rippu Shobo, 1986. Later films and all synopses by the author.

Harbor Toast: Victory is in Our Grasp / Minato no kanpai: shori o wagate ni (as Seitaro Suzuki)

1956, B&W, 65 min.
PRODUCER: Kanzo Asada
SCREENWRITER: Norio Nakagawa, Kiriro Urayama
CINEMATOGRAPHER: Kumenobu Fujioka
ART DIRECTOR: Koreyoshi Kurahar
MUSIC: Hideo Hiragawa
PRINCIPAL CAST: Ko Mishima, Shinsuke Maki, Sumiko Minami

Pure Emotions of the Sea / Hozuma wa utau: umi no junjo (as Seitaro Suzuki)

1956, B&W, 48 min.
PRODUCER: Ryoji Mogi
SCREENWRITER: Asami Tanabe, Norimasa Mayumi
CINEMATOGRAPHER: Kazue Nagatsuka
ART DIRECTOR: Kazuo Yagyu
MUSIC: Yashi Eguchi
PRINCIPAL CAST: Hachiro Kasuga, Jushiro Kobayashi, Toshie Takada

Satan's Town / Akuma no macho (as Seitaro Suzuki)

1956, B&W, 79 min.
PRODUCER: Takeo Yanagawa
SCREENWRITER: Goro Shiraishi
CINEMATOGRAPHER: Kazue Nagatsuka
ART DIRECTOR: Sanpei Satani
MUSIC: Taiichiro Kosugi
PRINCIPAL CAST: Seizaburo Kawatsu, Shinsuke Ashida, Ichiro Sugai
SYNOPSIS: A gangster is torn between remaining loyal to his crime boss and betraying him to the police before he can flee to Hong Kong. Includes early examples of visual tricks using reflective surfaces.

Inn of the Floating Weeds / Ukikasa no yado (as Seitaro Suzuki)

1957, B&W, 74 min.
PRODUCER: Ryoji Mogi
SCREENWRITER: Iwao Yamazaki
CINEMATOGRAPHER: Toshitato Nakao
ART DIRECTOR: Akiyoshi Satani
MUSIC: Yashi Eguchi
PRINCIPAL CAST: Hideaki Nitani, Hachiro Kasuga, Hisano Yamaoka

Eight Hours of Fear / Hachijikan no kyofu (as Seitaro Suzuki)

1957, B&W, 78 min.
PRODUCER: Kenzo Asada
SCREENWRITER: Goro Tanada, Rokuro Tsukiji
CINEMATOGRAPHER: Kazue Nagatsuka
ART DIRECTOR: Akiyoshi Satani
MUSIC: Takio Niki
PRINCIPAL CAST: Hideaki Nitani, Taizo Fukami, Eiko Misuzu, Keiko Shima
SYNOPSIS: When their train is trapped by a landslide, passengers, including a murderer being escorted to prison, must take a perilous bus ride through a remote area where two bank robbers are at large.

The Naked Woman and the Gun / Rajo to kenju (as Seitaro Suzuki)

1957, B&W, 88 min.
PRODUCER: Kenzo Asada
SCREENWRITER: Asami Tanabe
CINEMATOGRAPHER: Umeo Matsuhashi
ART DIRECTOR: Kazuhiko Chiba
MUSIC: Mutsuro Hara
PRINCIPAL CAST: Michitaro Mizushima, Mari Shiraki, Ichiro Sugai

Underworld Beauty / Ankokugai no bijo

1957, B&W, 87 min., Cinemascope
PRODUCER: Takashi Nishihara
SCREENWRITER: Kan Saji
CINEMATOGRAPHER: Toshitaro Nakao
ART DIRECTOR: Bugen Sakaguchi
MUSIC: Naozumi Yamamoto
PRINCIPAL CAST: Mari Shiraki, Michitaro Mizushima, Hideaki Nitani, Shinsuke Ashida
SYNOPSIS: A gangster's girlfriend is coerced into joining his diamond smuggling operation. Notable for Mari Shiraki's energetic performance in the title role. Suzuki's first film directed under his adopted name, Seijun Suzuki.

The Boy Who Made Good a.k.a. The Spring That Didn't Come / Fumihazushita haru

1958, B&W, 99 min., Cinemascope
PRODUCER: Masayuki Takagi
SCREENWRITER: Nobuyoshi Terada, Tatsumon Okada
CINEMATOGRAPHER: Yoshihiro Yamazaki
ART DIRECTOR: Kazuhiko Chiba
MUSIC: Hikaru Hayashi
PRINCIPAL CAST: Akira Kobayashi, Ruriko Asaoka, Sachiko Hidari
SYNOPSIS: A social worker tries to rehabilitate a teenager recently released from juvenile detention by awakening his passion for art. A scene in which a tour bus guide emphasizes the similarities among Tokyo, Paris, and New York highlights a contemporary fad for Western fashion. Includes early examples of Suzuki creatively using shoji screens as framing devices.

Young Breasts / Aoi chibusa

1958, B&W, 90 min., Cinemascope
PRODUCER: Takeshi Yamamato
SCREENWRITER: Hyogo Suzuki, Yoshiro Tsuji
CINEMATOGRAPHER: Kazue Nagatsuka
ART DIRECTOR: Kimihiko Nakamura
MUSIC: Yoshio Mamiya, Seiji Hiraoka
PRINCIPAL CAST: Akira Kobayashi, Misako Watanabe, Mihoko Inagaki
SYNOPSIS: Melodrama in which a troubled teen blackmails his father's new, young wife. He takes up with an innocent young woman, who is exploited by his juvenile delinquent friends.

The Voice without a Shadow / Kagenaki Koe

1958, B&W, 92 min., Cinemascope
PRODUCER: Kaneo Iwai
SCREENWRITER: Ryuta Akimoto, Kan Saji
CINEMATOGRAPHER: Kazue Nagatsuka
ART DIRECTOR: Bugen Sakaguchi
MUSIC: Hikaru Hayashi
PRINCIPAL CAST: Hideaki Nitani, Yoko Minamida, Jo Shishido

Love Letter / Rabu retaa

1959, B&W, 40 min., Cinemascope
PRODUCER: Kenzo Asada
SCREENWRITER: Kiichi Ishii
CINEMATOGRAPHER: Yu Kakita
ART DIRECTOR: Kazuo Yagyu
MUSIC: Yoshio Mamiya
PRINCIPAL CAST: Kyosuke Machida, Frankie Sakai, Hisako Tsukuba

Passport to Darkness / Ankoku no ryoken

1959, B&W, 89 min., Cinemascope
PRODUCER: Kenzo Asada
SCREENWRITER: Hajime Takaiwa
CINEMATOGRAPHER: Kazue Nagatsuka
MUSIC: Taiichiro Kosugi, Koichi Kawabe
PRINCIPAL CAST: Ryoji Hayama, Tamaki Sawa, Masumi Okada
SYNOPSIS: A film noir in which a trombonist's wife is kidnapped from a train. He finds her body in his apartment and must retrace his steps to determine who murdered her.

Features unconventional use of zooms and early experiments with composing shots in extreme depth.

Naked Age a.k.a Age of Nudity a.k.a. Age of Innocence / Suppadaka no nenrei

1959, B&W, 54 min., Cinemascope
PRODUCER: Hideo Koi
SCREENWRITER: Nobuyoshi Terada, Seijun Suzuki
CINEMATOGRAPHER: Kumenobu Fujioka
ART DIRECTOR: Bugen Sakaguchi
MUSIC: Michiaki Watanabe
PRINCIPAL CAST: Keiichiro Akagi, Kyoko Hori, Saburo Fujimaki
SYNOPSIS: Uncharacteristically (for Suzuki) tender story about street urchins, one of whom is trying to save himself by going to school. The only Nikkatsu film for which Suzuki received co-credit on the screenplay.

Take Aim at the Police Van / Sono gososha o nerae

1960, B&W, 79 min., Cinemascope
PRODUCER: Ryoji Mogi
SCREENWRITER: Shinichi Sekizawa
CINEMATOGRAPHER: Shigeyoshi Mine
PRINCIPAL CAST: Michitaro Mizushima, Misako Watanabe, Shoichi Ozawa
SYNOPSIS: After a prison transport truck is attacked and one of the prisoners murdered, the guard on duty is accused of negligence. He vows to track down the killers. Suzuki's first collaboration with cinematographer Shigeyoshi Mine, who would work with him on several more films at Nikkatsu. Interesting shots emphasize Tokyo's train and roadway infrastructure.

The Sleeping Beast Within a.k.a. The Sleep of the Beast / Kemono no nemuri

1960, B&W, 85 min., Cinemascope
PRODUCER: Takiko Mizunoe
SCREENWRITER: Ichiro Ikeda
CINEMATOGRAPHER: Shigeyoshi Mine
ART DIRECTOR: Kimihiko Nakamura
PRINCIPAL CAST: Hiroyuki Nagato, Shinsuke Ashida, Hisano Yamaoka
SYNOPSIS: When a traveling salesman goes missing, his daughter and a reporter discover that he's become involved in murder, heroin smuggling, and a mysterious Sun God cult.

Smashing the O-Line a.k.a. Clandestine Zero Line / Mikko zero line

1960, B&W, 83 min., Cinemascope
PRODUCER: Shozo Ashida
SCREENWRITER: Yasuro Yokoyama
CINEMATOGRAPHER: Shigeyoshi Mine, Toshitaro Nakao
ART DIRECTOR: Kazuhiko Chiba
PRINCIPAL CAST: Hiroyuki Nagato, Mayumi Shimizu, Yuji Odaka
SYNOPSIS: An amoral reporter disappears while on a story about drug smuggling and illegal immigration. His colleague goes undercover on an immigrant smuggling boat to search for him. Much darker, more nihilistic atmosphere than previous films.

Everything Goes Wrong a.k.a. The Precipice / Subete ga Kurutteru

1960, B&W, 72 min., Cinemascope
PRODUCER: Kenzo Asada
SCREENWRITER: Seiji Hoshigawa
CINEMATOGRAPHER: Izumi Hagiwara
ART DIRECTOR: Kazuhiko Chiba
MUSIC: Keitaro Miho
PRINCIPAL CAST: Tamio Kawachi, Tomoko Naraoka
SYNOPSIS: A teenager whose father died in World War II is resentful of his mother for marrying a man who worked for a weapons manufacturer and contrives to humiliate him. Contrast between indoor and outdoor scenes highlights Suzuki's facility with location shooting and boredom with normal indoor studio sets.

Fighting Delinquents / Kutabare gurentai

1960, color, 80 min., Cinemascope
PRODUCER: Hideo Koi
SCREENWRITER: Iwao Yamazaki
CINEMATOGRAPHER: Kazue Nagatsuka
ART DIRECTOR: Akiyoshi Satani
MUSIC: Sietaro Omori

PRINCIPAL CAST: Koji Wada, Mayumi Shimizu, Yasuhiro Kameyama

Tokyo Knights / Tokyo Kishitai a.k.a. Tokyo Naito

1961, color, 81 min., Cinemascope
PRODUCER: Hideo Koi
SCREENWRITER: Iwao Yamazaki
CINEMATOGRAPHER: Kazue Nagatsuka
ART DIRECTOR: Kimihiko Nakamura
MUSIC: Seitaro Omuri
PRINCIPAL CAST: Koji Wada, Mayumi Shimizu, Yoko Minamida

The Big Boss Who Needs No Gun / Muteppo taisho

1961, color, 82 min., Cinemascope
PRODUCER: Keinosuke Kubo
SCREENWRITER: Kenro Matsuura, Ryuzo Nakanishi
CINEMATOGRAPHER: Kazue Nagatsuka
ART DIRECTOR: Toshiyuki Matsui
MUSIC: So Kaburagi
PRINCIPAL CAST: Koji Wada, Mitsuo Sagawa, Mayumi Shimizu

The Man with a Shotgun / Sandanju no otoko a.k.a Shottogan no otoko

1961, color, 84 min., Cinemascope
PRODUCER: Kaneo Iwai
SCREENWRITER: Kenro Matsuura, Kiichi Ishii
CINEMATOGRAPHER: Shigeyoshi Mine
ART DIRECTOR: Akiyoshi Satari
MUSIC: Masayoshi Ikeda
PRINCIPAL CAST: Hideaki Nitani, Izumi Ashikawa, Yuji Odaka
SYNOPSIS: A hunter comes upon a mountain village where the residents elect him sheriff to search for a killer. An adventure story mimicking American Westerns in style and look. Suzuki and cinematographer Shigeyoshi Mine experiment with eccentric use of depth-of-field and compositions incorporating reflections.

The Breeze on the Ridge a.k.a. The Wind-of-Youth Group Crosses the Mountain Pass / Toge o wataru wakai kaze

1961, color, 85 min., Cinemascope
PRODUCER: Takeo Yanagawa
SCREENWRITER: Ichiro Ikeda, Fumi Takahashi, Yoshihiko Morimoto
CINEMATOGRAPHER: Saburo Isayama
ART DIRECTOR: Kazuhiko Chiba
MUSIC: Seitaro Omori
PRINCIPAL CAST: Koji Wada, Mayumi Shimizu, Chiyoko Shimakura
SYNOPSIS: A student hitches a ride with an itinerant variety show making the rounds of summer festivals. When the star exotic dancer quits, the student helps the troupe revamp their act. Notable for a scene in which colored liquids are thrown onto the screen and tint the entire scene: an early example of Suzuki experimenting with unorthodox visual effects.

The Blood-Red Channel a.k.a. Blood-Red Water in the Channel / Kaikyo, chi ni somete

1961, color, 84 min., Cinemascope
PRODUCER: Shozo Ashida, Hideo Koi
SCREENWRITER: Goro Tanada
CINEMATOGRAPHER: Shigeyoshi Mine
ART DIRECTOR: Kimihiko Nakamura
MUSIC: Seitaro Omori
PRINCIPAL CAST: Koji Wada, Ryoji Hayama, Mayumi Shimizu
SYNOPSIS: Two brothers from a small island take opposite paths in life: one becomes a Coast Guard officer and the other a smuggler. Lack of energy shows Suzuki struggling with a weak script and an unfamiliar rural environment far from the Tokyo settings in which he thrives.

Million Dollar Smash-and-Grab / Hyakuman doru o tatakidase

1961, color, 90 min., Cinemascope
PRODUCER: Shizo Ashida
SCREENWRITER: Naohachi Tagi
CINEMATOGRAPHER: Shigeyoshi Mine
ART DIRECTOR: Kimihiko Nakamura
MUSIC: Hajime Okumura

PRINCIPAL CAST: Koji Wada, Keisuke Noro, Misako Watanabe
SYNOPSIS: Two boxers move from a small town to Tokyo. Once gets involved with yakuza. The other becomes a pawn in a battle between his old-fashioned manager and a better-funded one who wants to poach him. Notable for an early example of Suzuki using sudden wind effects to externalize characters' emotions.

Teenage Yakuza / High-Teen Yakuza

1962, B&W, 72 min., Cinemascope
PRODUCER: Jiro Tomoda
SCREENWRITER: Nozomu Yoshimura, Mamoru Okuzono
CINEMATOGRAPHER: Kenji Hagiwara
ART DIRECTOR: Kazuhiko Chiba
MUSIC: Harumi Ibe
PRINCIPAL CAST: Tamio Kawachi, Kayo Matsuko, Noriko Matsumoto
SYNOPSIS: Incongruously comedic-toned story of teenage yakuza terrorizing shop owners and the good kids who oppose them.

The Guys Who Put Money on Me / Ore ni kaketa yatsura

1962, color, 90 min., Cinemascope
PRODUCER: Takeshi Yamamoto
SCREENWRITER: Ei Ogawa, Kensho Nakano
CINEMATOGRAPHER: Shigeyoshi Mine
ART DIRECTOR: Bugen Sakaguchi
MUSIC: Seitaro Omori
PRINCIPAL CAST: Koji Wada, Ryoji Hayama, Tamio Kawachi

Detective Bureau 2-3: Go To Hell, Bastards! / Tantei jimusho 23: Katubare akutodomo

1963, color, 89 min., Cinemascope
PRODUCER: Shozo Ashida
SCREENWRITER: Iwao Yamazaki
CINEMATOGRAPHER: Shigeyoshi Mine
ART DIRECTOR: Bugen Sakaguchi
MUSIC: Harumi Ibe
PRINCIPAL CAST: Jo Shishido, Reiko Sasamori, Naomi Hoshi
SYNOPSIS: A cocky cop goes undercover to infiltrate a gang and find their cache of stolen weapons. Unconventional camerawork and action scenes indicate the beginning of Suzuki's most creative Nikkatsu phase. Suzuki's first film with actor Jo Shishido, a frequent collaborator.

Youth of the Beast / Yaju no seishun

1963, color, 92 min., Cinemascope
PRODUCER: Keinosuke Kubo
SCREENWRITER: Ichiro Ikeda, Tadaaki Yamazaki
CINEMATOGRAPHER: Kazue Nagatsuka
ART DIRECTOR: Karyo Yokoo
MUSIC: Hajime Okumura
PRINCIPAL CAST: Jo Shishido, Tamio Kawaji, Misako Watanabe
SYNOPSIS: A disgraced former cop avenges the death of his partner by infiltrating two rival yakuza gangs and setting them against each other. Considered a major creative breakthrough for its famous one-way mirror nightclub scene and other striking uses of color, camerawork, and action choreography.

Bastard / Akutaro

1963, B&W, 95 min., Cinemascope
PRODUCER: Masayuki Takagi
SCREENWRITER: Ryozo Kasahara
CINEMATOGRAPHER: Shigeyoshi Mine
ART DIRECTOR: Takeo Kimura
MUSIC: Hajime Okumura
PRINCIPAL CAST: Ken Yamauchi, Masako Izumi, Midori Tashiro

Kanto Wanderer / Kanto Mushuku

1963, color, 93 min., Cinemascope
PRODUCER: Kenzo Asada
SCREENWRITER: Yasutaro Yagi
CINEMATOGRAPHER: Shigeyoshi Mine
ART DIRECTOR: Takeo Kimura
MUSIC: Masayoshi Ikeda
PRINCIPAL CAST: Akira Kobayashi, Chieko Matsubara, Hiroko Ito
SYNOPSIS: When a yakuza bodyguard meets a mysterious woman from his past, he is torn between his desire for her and performing his duty for his boss. Notable for its unorthodox use of color and theatrical lighting effects, and a famous Kabuki-inspired fight scene in

which shoji screens fall away to reveal a wall of pure red light.

The Flower and the Angry Waves / Hana to doto

1964, color, 92 min., Cinemascope
PRODUCER: Takeo Yanagawa
SCREENWRITER: Kazuo Funabashi, Keiichi Abe, Takeo Kimura
CINEMATOGRAPHER: Kazue Nagatsuka
ART DIRECTOR: Takeo Kimura
MUSIC: Hajime Okumura
PRINCIPAL CAST: Akira Kobayashi, Chieko Matsubara, Osamu Takizawa

Gate of Flesh / Nikutai no mon

1964, color, 90 min., Cinemascope
PRODUCER: Kaneo Iwai
SCREENWRITER: Goro Tanada
CINEMATOGRAPHER: Shigeyoshi Mine
ART DIRECTOR: Takeo Kimura
MUSIC: Naozumi Yamamoto
PRINCIPAL CAST: Jo Shishido, Yumiko Nogawa, Kayo Matsuo
SYNOPSIS: The lives of four prostitutes in postwar Tokyo are disrupted when a former soldier takes refuge in their underground lair. Based on a famous novel by Taijiro Tamura espousing the pursuit of erotic pleasure over fealty to authority. Contains Suzuki's most experimental use of superimpositions.

The Call of Blood a.k.a. Our Blood Won't Allow It / Oretachi no chi ga yurusanai

1964, color, 97 min., Cinemascope
PRODUCER: Masayuko Takagi
SCREENWRITER: Ryuma Takemuri, Katsuhiro Hosomi, Michiko Ikezawa
CINEMATOGRAPHER: Shigeyoshi Mine
ART DIRECTOR: Takeo Kimura
MUSIC: Tadanori Suzuki, Hiroshi Ikezawa
PRINCIPAL CAST: Akira Kobayashi, Hideki Takahishi, Chieko Matsubara

Story of a Prostitute a.k.a. Joy Girls / Shunpuden

1965, B&W, 96 min., Cinemascope
PRODUCER: Kaneo Iwai
SCREENWRITER: Hajime Takaiwa
CINEMATOGRAPHER: Kazue Nagatsuka
ART DIRECTOR: Takeo Kimura
MUSIC: Naozumi Yamamoto
PRINCIPAL CAST: Tamio Kawachi, Yumiko Nogawa, Kayo Matsuo
SYNOPSIS: A comfort woman sent to the front lines during the Sino-Japanese War falls in love with a young lieutenant. They must hide their affair from the senior officer, who considers her his exclusive property. Based on a Taijiro Tamura novel that was previously made into the film *Escape at Dawn*, directed by Akira Kurosawa.

Born under Crossed Stars / Akutaroden: warui-hoshi no shita demo

1965, B&W, 98 min., Cinemascope
PRODUCER: Masayuki Takagi
SCREENWRITER: Ryozo Kasahara
CINEMATOGRAPHER: Kazue Nagatsuka
ART DIRECTOR: Takeo Kimura
MUSIC: Hajime Okumura
PRINCIPAL CAST: Ken Yamauchi, Jun Tatara, Masako Izumi
SYNOPSIS: Comedic love story about a teenage milk salesman torn between a good girl and a bad girl. Suzuki uses exaggerated comedic effects such as loud kissing noises during a make-out session and a monkey in a baby carriage.

Tattooed Life / Irezumi ichidai

1965, color, 87 min., Cinemascope
PRODUCER: Masayuki Takagi
SCREENWRITER: Kinya Naoi, Kei Hattori
CINEMATOGRAPHER: Kurataro Takamura
ART DIRECTOR: Takeo Kimura
MUSIC: Masayoshi Ikeda
PRINCIPAL CAST: Hideki Takahashi, Hiroko Ito, Asako Izumi
SYNOPSIS: A yakuza hit man and his peaceful younger brother go on the run after the latter kills a rival. Most famous for its final flight scene, part of which is filmed from below a suddenly invisible floor. Its stylistic excesses led Suzuki's bosses to warn him that he was "going too far."

Carmen from Kawachi / Kawachi Carmen

1966, B&W, 89 min., Cinemascope
PRODUCER: Seijaku Sakaue
SCREENWRITER: Katsumi Miki
CINEMATOGRAPHER: Shigeyoshi Mine
ART DIRECTOR: Takeo Kimura
MUSIC: Taichiro Kosugi
PRINCIPAL CAST: Yumiko Nogawa, Tamio Kawachi, Chikako Miyagi
SYNOPSIS: Melodrama about a woman who moves from a small town to Osaka to work as a bargirl. She experiences a series of misadventures with men, including a former boyfriend, a wealthy tycoon, and an abusive priest.

Tokyo Drifter a.k.a. The Man from Tokyo / Tokyo Nagramono

1966, color, 89 min., Cinemascope
PRODUCER: Tetsuo Nakagawa
SCREENWRITER: Yasunori Kawauchi
CINEMATOGRAPHER: Shigeyoshi Mine
ART DIRECTOR: Takeo Kimura
MUSIC: So Kaburagi
PRINCIPAL CAST: Tatsuya Watari, Chieko Matsubara, Hideaki Nitani
SYNOPSIS: A yakuza is pursued by hit men when he tries to leave his life of crime behind. Intended as a promotional vehicle to showcase actor/singer Tetsuya Watari and the film's title song. Suzuki and art director Takeo Kimura made creative use of minimal sets and emphasized the absurdity of the film's plot through comic action scenes.

Fighting Elegy a.k.a. The Born Fighter / Kenka erejii

1966, B&W, 86 min., Cinemascope
PRODUCER: Kazu Otsuka
SCREENWRITER: Kaneto Shindo
CINEMATOGRAPHER: Kenji Hagiwara
ART DIRECTOR: Takeo Kimura
MUSIC: Takeharu Yamamoto
PRINCIPAL CAST: Hideki Takahashi, Junko Asano, Yusuke Kawatsu
SYNOPSIS: A teenager who suppresses his lustful impulses by fighting is conscripted into the army. Suzuki altered the script by adding a scene with war propagandist Kita Ikki and having the hero go to the front of the Sino-Japanese War at the end.

Branded to Kill / Koroshi no rakuin

1967, B&W, 91 min., Cinemascope
PRODUCER: Kaneo Iwai
SCREENWRITER: Guryu Hachiro
CINEMATOGRAPHER: Kazue Nagatsuka
ART DIRECTOR: Takeo Kimura
MUSIC: Naozumi Yamamoto
PRINCIPAL CAST: Jo Shishido, Mariko Ogawa, Annu Mari
SYNOPSIS: A hit man tries to work his way up the ranks of his assassins' organization by killing those above him. Suzuki's most extreme use of fragmented narrative, odd camera angles, rapid editing, and hysterical acting thus far. Script credited to *Guryu Hachiro*, a group of eight of Suzuki's regular crew members, including Takeo Kimura. Led to Suzuki's firing by Nikkatsu.

A Tale of Sorrow and Sadness / Hishu Monogatari

1977, color, 91 min., Cinemascope
PRODUCER: Ikki Kajiwara, Yutaka Fujioka, Yasuhiko Kawano, Kenzo Asano, Yoshiki Nomura
SCREENWRITER: Atsushi Yamatoya
CINEMATOGRAPHER: Masaru Mori
MUSIC: Keitaro Miho, Ichiro Tomita
PRINCIPAL CAST: Yoko Shiraki, Yoshio Harada, Masumi Okada
SYNOPSIS: A model is trained to become a professional golfer as a publicity stunt, but a run-in with a deranged fan leads to a blackmail plot. Suzuki's return to directing after a ten-year hiatus caused by collusion among the five major studios.

Zigeunerweisen

1980, color, 145 min.
PRODUCER: Genjiro Arato
SCREENWRITER: Yozo Tanaka
CINEMATOGRAPHER: Kazue Nagatsuka
ART DIRECTOR: Takeo Kimura
MUSIC: Osamu Kawachi

PRINCIPAL CAST: Toshiya Fujita, Michiyu Okusu, Yoshio Harada, Naoko Otani
SYNOPSIS: Two former academic colleagues meet by chance in a seaside town and become involved in a series of mysterious incidents. Suzuki's first independent film and the first of his trilogy set in the Taisho era. Voted the best Japanese film of the 1980s by Japanese film critics.

Kagero-za a.k.a. Heat-Haze Theatre

1981, color, 139 min.
PRODUCER: Genjiro Arato
SCREENWRITER: Yozo Tanaka
CINEMATOGRAPHER: Kazue Nagatsuka
ART DIRECTOR: Senkoku Iketani
MUSIC: Osamu Kawachi
PRINCIPAL CAST: Yusaku Matsuda, Michiyo Okusu, Mariko Kaga, Yoshio Harada, Kazuo Nakamura
SYNOPSIS: A wealthy arts patron attempts to engineer a suicide pact between his wife and a young playwright. The second film in the Taisho Trilogy.

Capone Cries A Lot a.k.a. Kaiemon / Kapone oi ni naku

1985, color, 130 min., VistaVision
PRODUCER: Goro Sakurai, Kenichi Nakamura
SCREENWRITER: Atsushi Yamatoya, Takeo Kimura, Koichi Suzuki
CINEMATOGRAPHER: Akira Takada, Junichi Fujisawa
ART DIRECTOR: Takeo Kimura, Yuji Maruyama
MUSIC: Takayuki Inoue
PRINCIPAL CAST: Kenichi Hagiwara, Yuko Tanaka, Akira Emoto, Kenji Sawada
SYNOPSIS: A traditional *naniwa-bushi* singer moves to Prohibition-era San Francisco to try to become a star in America.

Lupin III: Legend of the Gold of Babylon / Rupan sansei, babyron no ogon densetsu

1985, color, animation, 100 min.
PRODUCER: Tetsuo Katayama, Kazushichi Sano, Hidehiko Takei
CO-DIRECTOR: Shigetsugu Yoshida
SCREENWRITER: Yoshio Urasawa, Atsushi Yamatoya
CINEMATOGRAPHER: Hajime Hasegawa
MUSIC: Yuji Ohno

Yumeji

1991, color, 128 min.
PRODUCER: Genjiro Arato
SCREENWRITER: Yozo Tanaka
CINEMATOGRAPHER: Junichi Fujisawa
ART DIRECTOR: Noriyoshi Ikeya
MUSIC: Kaname Kawachi, Shigeru Umebayashi
PRINCIPAL CAST: Kenji Sawada, Tomoko Mariya, Tamasaburo Bando
SYNOPSIS: Fictionalized adventures of the painter Takehisa Yumeji. The final film in the Taisho trilogy.

Pistol Opera / Pisutoru Opera

2001, color, 112 min.
PRODUCER: Ikki Katashima, Satoru Ogura
SCREENWRITER: Kazunori Ito, Takeo Kimura
CINEMATOGRAPHER: Yonezo Maeda
ART DIRECTOR: Takeo Kimura
MUSIC: Kazufumi Kodama
PRINCIPAL CAST: Makiko Esumi, Sayoko Yamaguchi, Kirin Kiki, Mikijiro Hira
SYNOPSIS: A variation on the plot of *Branded to Kill* with a female killer battling the other members of her assassins guild.

Princess Raccoon / Operetta tanuki goten

2005, color, 111 min.
PRODUCER: Nobuyuki Tohya, Satoru Ogura, Ikki Katashima
SCREENWRITER: Yoshio Urasawa
CINEMATOGRAPHER: Yonezo Maeda
ART DIRECTOR: Takeo Kimura
MUSIC: Michiru Oshima, Ryomei Shirai
PRINCIPAL CAST: Zhang Ziyi, Joe Odagiri, Hiroko Yakushimaru, Saori Yuki
SYNOPSIS: Musical fantasy about a prince who falls in love with a shape-shifting raccoon spirit.

APPENDIX 2

Biographical Chronology

Years 1923–90 compiled by Shigehiko Hasumi in *De woestijn onder de kersenbloesem—The Desert under the Cherry Blossoms* (Abcoude: Uitgeverij Uniepers). Years 1992 through the present compiled by the author.

1923 May 24, born in Nihonbashi, the center of Tokyo, as Seitaro Suzuki. His family is in the textile trade. Often participates in track meets as a short-distance runner in primary school.

1941 Earns his degree from Tokyo Trade School. Fails the entrance exam for a special vocational college.

1943 Called up to fight at the front; becomes a private second class.

1944 Sent to the southern front by cargo ship. The fleet is destroyed in an attack by an American submarine, and Suzuki flees to the Philippines. Takes a freighter to Taiwan, but the ship sinks after being attacked by the American air force. Floats around until he is rescued.

1946 Fails the entrance exam for Tokyo University and enrolls in the film department of Kamakura Academy. Passes the assistant director's exam for Shochiku Ofuna studios and becomes a regular employee. Monthly salary increases from 15,000 to 40,000 yen.

1949 Works as assistant director on a film by Minoru Shibuya. Serves as an assistant in Tsuruo Iwama's group for the next four years while occasionally publishing screenplays.

1954 Moves to the reopened Nikkatsu Studios and continues as an assistant director, in Hiroshi Noguchi's group.

1955 His screenplay *Rakujitsu no ketto* (*Duel at Sunset*) is filmed, directed by Hiroshi Noguchi.

1958 Directs *Ankokugai no bijou* (*Underworld Beauty*), his first film as Seijun Suzuki, and goes on to direct three or four films per year.

1963 Wins the confidence of the studio heads with *Akutaro* (*Bastard*).

1966 Becomes the subject of an increasing number of articles, interviews, and essays in film magazines.

1967 Enrages Nikkatsu's president Kyusaku Hori with *Koroshi no rakuin* (*Branded to Kill*).

1968 Starts shooting the series *Aisaikun konbanwa, aru ketto* (*Good Evening Dear Husband—a Duel*) for Nikkatsu's TV division. Is informed by Nikkatsu's head office in April that he's been fired because his films are "incomprehensible"; distribution of his films is stopped. A group forms to support Suzuki. Sues Nikkatsu in June; in July, the first public hearing takes place.

1969 Prevented from making films because of an agreement between the five major studios. Earns his living by making commercials, for which he wins an award the same year. The broadcasting of his TV film *Otoko no naka niwa tori ga iru* (*There's a Bird Inside a Man*) is cancelled because of problems with the sponsors.

1970 Publishes *Kenka erejii* (*Fighting Elegy*), which contains the script of the film and a number of poems.

1971 The lawsuit ends in a settlement. Hori leaves Nikkatsu.

1972 Publishes *Hanajigoku* (*Flowerhell*).

1973 Publishes *Boryokusagashi ni macho e deru* (*Going Into Town Looking for Violence*).

1975 Publishes *Hana to Kitoshi* (*The Flower and the Faith Healer*). Guest appearance in Kazuki Omori's *Kuraku nary made matenai* (*I Can't Wait Until Dark*).

1977 Shochiku releases *Hishu Monogatari* (*A Tale of Sorrow and Sadness*), his first film in ten years.

1980 Cinema Placet, Suzuki's own film company, produces and releases *Zigeunerweisen*. Starts to act more often in TV films. Publishes *Koshu* (*Lonely Reflections*).

1981 *Zigeunerweisen* is shown at the Berlin Film Festival and awarded a Special Jury Mention.

1982 Publishes *Machizukushi* (*A Catalogue of Cities*).

1984 Invited to the Pesaro Film Festival, the first retrospective of his work in a foreign country.

1985 Elected "Best Dressed Man" by the Japan Fashion Society.

1986 Koshi Ueno publishes *Suzuki Seijun, zen-eiga* (*Suzuki Seijun, All His Films*).

1994 *Branded to Thrill: The Delirious Cinema of Suzuki Seijun*, a fourteen-film retrospective organized by the British Film Institute, begins touring Europe and North America, giving his films their first major exposure in those areas.

2001 Returns to filmmaking after another ten-year hiatus with *Pistol Opera*. Nikkatsu presents *Style to Kill*, a twenty-film retrospective, in Tokyo.

2005 Directs *Princess Raccoon*, starring Zhang Ziyi and Joe Odagiri.

2006 Declares in an interview that he will not direct any more films due to his poor health. Nikkatsu presents another retrospective, *The Suzuki Seijun 48 Film Challenge*, at the Tokyo International Film Festival.

2008 Attends the Tokyo Project Gathering, an international coproduction market, to pitch a new film titled *A Goldfish of the Flame*.

Bibliography

Berra, J. (ed.), *Directory of World Cinema: Japan*, Bristol: Intellect Books, 2010.

Bordwell, D., *Planet Hong Kong: Popular Cinema and the Art of Entertainment*, Cambridge: Harvard University Press, 2000.

Branded to Kill, dir. Suzuki, S., Japan, Nikkatsu, [DVD].

Brody, R., "A Few Thoughts on Vulgar Auteurism," *The New Yorker*, http://www.newyorker.com/online/blogs/movies/2013/06/vulgar-auteurism-history-of-new-wave-cinema.html

Brown, K., and S. Minichiello, *Taisho Chic*, Honolulu: Honolulu Academy of Arts, 1995.

Burch, N., *To the Distant Observer: Form and Meaning in the Japanese Cinema*, Berkeley: University of California Press, 1979.

Chiaki, A., J. Clark, J. Menzies, and T. Mizusawa, *Modern Boy Modern Girl: Modernity in Japanese Art 1910 – 1935*, New South Wales: Art Gallery of New South Wales, 1998.

Desjardins, C., *Outlaw Masters of Japanese Film*, London: I.B. Tauris & Co. Ltd., 2005.

Dower, J., *Embracing Defeat: Japan in the Wake of World War II*, New York: W. W. Norton & Company, Inc., 1999.

Ebert, R., "'All War Stories are Told by Survivors': An Interview with Sam Fuller," http://www.rogerebert.com/interviews/all-war-stories-are-told-by-survivors-an-interview-with-samuel-fuller

Eco, U., *The Open Work*, trans. A. Cancogni, Cambridge: Harvard University Press, 1989.

Fields, S. (ed.), and T. Rayns, *Branded to Thrill: The Delirious Cinema of Suzuki Seijun*, London: British Film Institute, 1995.

Gate of Flesh, dir. Suzuki, S., Japan, Nikkatsu, 1964 [DVD].

Hampton, H., "*Youth of the Beast*: Screaming Target," *The Criterion Collection*, http://www.criterion.com/current/posts/351-youth-of-the-beast-screaming-target

Hasumi, S. (ed.), *De woestijn onder de kersenbloesem—The Desert under the Cherry Blossoms*, Abcoude: Uitgeverij Uniepers, 1991.

Hayman D., D. Michaelis, G. Plimpton, and R. Rhodes, "Kurt Vonnegut: The Art of Fiction No. 64," *The Paris Review*, http://www.theparisreview.org/interviews/3605/the-art-of-fiction-no-64-kurt-vonnegut

Hoffman, M., "The Taisho Era: When Modernity Ruled Japan's Masses," *The Japan Times*, http://www.japantimes.co.jp/life/2012/07/29/general/the-taisho-era-when-modernity-ruled-japans-masses/#.Uoo_U-b3dbw

Kaneda, M., "A Very Brief History of the Sogetsu Art Center," http://post.at.moma.org/content_items/154-a-very-brief-history-of-the-sogetsu-art-center

Kawabata, Y., *Palm-of-the-Hand Stories*, trans. L. Dunlop and J. Holman, New York: Farrar, Straus and Giroux, 1988.

Kyoka, I., *In Light of Shadows: More Gothic Tales by Izumi Kyoka*, trans. C. Inouye, Honolulu: University of Hawaii Press, 2005.

Mars-Jones, A., *Noriko Smiling*, London: Notting Hill Editions, 2011.

McClintock, P., "Cannes 2012: John Woo Set to Remake Classic Japanese Mafia Pic 'Youth of the Beast,'" http://www.hollywoodreporter.com/news/cannes-john-woo-youth-of-beast-325524

McKenna, K., "Eno: Voyages in Time & Perception," *Musician*, http://music.hyperreal.org/artists/brian_eno/interviews/musn82.htm

Mes, T., "Japan Cult Cinema Interview: Seijun Suzuki," *Midnighteye*, http://www.midnighteye.com/interviews/seijun-suzuki/

Mes, T., "Yasuzo Masumura: Passion and Excess," *Midnighteye*, http://www.midnighteye.com/features/yasuzo-masumura-passion-and-excess/

Mes, T., and J. Sharp, *The Midnight Eye Guide to Japanese Film*, Berkeley: Stone Bridge Press, 2005.

Monk, K., "Japanese legend sees himself as simple chronicler," http://sweetbottom.tripod.com/Articles/Oct161991.html

Ortolani, B., *The Japanese Theatre*, Princeton: Princeton University Press, 1995.

Phillips, A. (ed.) and J. Stringer (ed.), *Japanese Cinema: Texts and Contexts*, London: Routledge, 2007.

Quentin Tarantino Archives, "*Kill Bill* References Guide," http://wiki.tarantino.info/index.php/Kill_Bill_References_Guide/japanese#Tokyo_Drifter_.281966.29

Richie, D., *A Hundred Years of Japanese Film*, Tokyo: Kodansha International Ltd., 2001.

Rose, S., "Man on the Moon," *The Guardian*, http://www.theguardian.com/film/2006/jun/30/1

Ruiz, R., *Poetics of Cinema*, trans. B. Holmes, Paris: Editions Dis Voir, 1995.

Sato, T., *Currents in Japanese Cinema*, trans. G. Barrett, New York: Kodansha America, Inc., 1987.

Schilling, M., *No Borders No Limits: Nikkatsu Action Cinema*, Godalming: FAB Press Ltd., 2007.

Schilling, M., *The Yakuza Movie Book*, Berkeley: Stone Bridge Press, 2003.

Scott, R., "Early Pop Guns," *The Times*, http://sweetbottom.tripod.com/Articles/Oct151994.htm

Screech, T., *Sex and the Floating World: Erotic Images in Japan 1700–1820*, London: Reaktion Books, 2009.

Seidensticker, E., *Low City, High City*, New York: Alfred A. Knopf, 1983.

Sharp, J., "A Tale of Sorrow and Sadness," *Midnighteye*, http://www.midnighteye.com/reviews/story-of-sorrow-and-sadness/

Silverberg, M., *Erotic Grotesque Nonsense: The Mass Culture of Japanese Modern Times*, Berkeley: University of California Press, 2009.

Standish, I., *A New History of Japanese Cinema*, New York: The Continuum International Publishing Group, 2006.

Stephens, C., "Takeo Kimura: 1918–2010," *The Criterion Collection*, http://www.criterion.com/current/posts/1433-takeo-kimura-1918-2010

Story of a Prostitute, dir. Suzuki, S., Japan, Nikkatsu, 1965, [DVD].

Suzuki, S., P. Willemen, and T. Sato, *The Films of Seijun Suzuki*, Edinburgh: Edinburgh Film Festival, 1988.

Tanizaki, J., *Naomi*, trans. A. Chambers, New York: Vintage International, 1985.

Teo, S., "Seijun Suzuki: Authority in Minority," *Senses of Cinema*, http://sensesofcinema.com/2000/festival-reports/suzuki/

Tokyo Drifter, dir. Suzuki, S., Japan, Nikkatsu, 1966, [DVD].

Toole, M., "The Mike Toole Show: The Lupin Tapes," http://www.animenews-network.com/the-mike-toole-show/the-lupin-tapes/2010-06-06

Tucker, P., "Predicting the Future with Phone Data and Tweets," *The Kojo Nnamdi Show*, http://thekojonnamdishow.org/shows/2014-07-08/predicting-future-phone-data-and-tweets

Wilonsky, R., "The Way of Jim Jarmusch," *Miami New Times*, http://www.miaminewtimes.com/film/the-way-of-jim-jarmusch-6356787

Youth of the Beast, dir. Suzuki, S., Japan, Nikkatsu, 1963, [DVD].

Index